ROUTLEDGE LIBRARY EDITIONS: WELFARE AND THE STATE

Volume 7

THE UNEMPLOYMENT SERVICES

THE UNEMPLOYMENT SERVICES

A Report Prepared for the Fabian Society

POLLY HILL

Routledge
Taylor & Francis Group
LONDON AND NEW YORK

First published in 1940 by George Routledge and Sons, Ltd.

This edition first published in 2019
by Routledge
2 Park Square, Milton Park, Abingdon, Oxon OX14 4RN

and by Routledge
711 Third Avenue, New York, NY 10017

Routledge is an imprint of the Taylor & Francis Group, an informa business

British Library Cataloguing in Publication Data
A catalogue record for this book is available from the British Library

ISBN: 978-1-138-61373-7 (Set)
ISBN: 978-0-429-45813-2 (Set) (ebk)
ISBN: 978-1-138-60127-7 (Volume 7) (hbk)
ISBN: 978-0-429-47008-0 (Volume 7) (ebk)

THE UNEMPLOYMENT SERVICES

A Report prepared for the Fabian Society

BY

POLLY HILL

FOREWORD BY

D. R. GRENFELL, M.P.

LONDON

GEORGE ROUTLEDGE & SONS, LTD.

BROADWAY HOUSE, 68–74 CARTER LANE, E.C.

First published 1940

Printed in Great Britain by Butler & Tanner Ltd., Frome and London

CONTENTS

FOREWORD

In this book Miss Hill has brought out something new and has added to a most thorough examination of the various sections of our system of unemployment relief a number of fundamental proposals for the extension of necessary provisions for improving the conditions of the unemployed and their dependants. She has shown a mastery of the existing law unusual in books of this type. Her knowledge of regulations and scales is equal to her original and unorthodox dissection of the principles embodied in this code of laws which plays so large a part in the lives of industrial workers and their dependants. This is not to be regarded as an explanatory pamphlet, although it does explain far more fully than anything I have read on the subject. It is a big work with a minimum of words to cover an immense scope.

Miss Hill has rightly called attention to the future and to the increase in unemployment that will occur almost overnight when the war industries close down and war personnel is demobilised. It is well that those who have to deal with unemployment as a political question should read this little book. I would strongly recommend the work to all my colleagues in the movement and would like to congratulate the author upon her success in this very difficult field of work.

D. R. GRENFELL, M.P.

HOUSE OF COMMONS.
December, 1939.

THIS report on the unemployment services was written for the Fabian Society in conjunction with one of its Committees in Oxford. The author is indebted to members of the Committee for help that was received from them and also to a large number of experts—both economists and administrators—who read the report and made detailed comments on it.

Both the work for this report and the writing of it was made possible by the great generosity of an anonymous member of the Fabian Society.

The Fabian Society has, of course, no collective responsibility for the views that are here expressed.

FABIAN SOCIETY,
11 DARTMOUTH ST.,
S.W.1.

December, 1939.

INTRODUCTION

THIS book is concerned with the changes that should be made in the unemployment insurance scheme and the Unemployment Assistance Board in a Labour Government's next term of office. The proposals that are made are appropriate only to the period of transition to socialism—to Labour's Immediate Programme—and will be completely out of date when a socialist system is finally set up. In considering one of the changing factors in a period of general change it is impossible to draw up a working list of priorities—to decide which of the many important changes will be made first—because this must depend to such a large extent upon the actual political atmosphere of the time. The unemployment services are therefore considered against the background of a capitalist system not radically different in structure from the present one.

Owing to the prevalence of unemployment every advanced capitalist state has been compelled to set up an intricate system of national social services to make some provision for the unemployed. These unemployment services have to be elaborate in order that they may be inserted as innocuously as possible into a structure of private enterprise ; and our British system of unemployment insurance and unemployment assistance is one of the most ingeniously constructed of them all. The system must be such that it does not reduce the supply of labour willing to work at a low wage ; it must not interfere with the individual's natural inclination to provide for future misfortune (even if that inclination results in present poverty) ; and it must generally be consistent with the idea that men only work in order to earn their living, and with the incentive of insecurity. The advantage of such a system is that it enables the Government to satisfy its natural humanitarian impulses and at the same time to ensure that the excess labour supply shall be immediately available when required.

But though we assume the capitalist background to be given, we do not also assume that the primary aim of all unemployment policy should be to respect this background. The background must compel us to compromise, but it must not hold us back all along the line. It is never possible to disclose all one's implicit assumptions, but the more important ones in this case are merely that widespread unemployment is a necessary feature of present-day capitalism, and thus (though not to the same degree) of the transition to socialism; the unemployed are not individually to blame for their plight; the State bears more than an ultimate responsibility for keeping all members of the community above the subsistence level.

In general the plan has been followed in this book of only discussing those aspects of the unemployment services that are most obviously unsatisfactory. Consequently the book is only incidentally descriptive, and some important, but relatively satisfactory, features of the two services go undiscussed. An attempt has been made to consider the unemployment insurance scheme and the Unemployment Assistance Board in conjunction with one another, and to avoid the usual tendency to consider the separate social services in complete isolation from one another. This tendency is contrary to the interests of the workers because it ignores the importance of uniformity of treatment for the individual throughout his various vicissitudes, and because it produces unfairness as between individuals.

THE UNEMPLOYMENT SERVICES

CHAPTER I

AN OUTLINE OF THE UNEMPLOYMENT SERVICES

BEFORE the plan of this book is outlined, the existing system of unemployment services will be very briefly described. The system is a "dual system" consisting of two absolutely distinct services, both of which are concerned with maintaining the unemployed. Under the unemployment insurance scheme [1] benefit is paid at a fixed rate to a limited class of insured people. The Unemployment Assistance Board relieves the actual need that arises out of unemployment, and is, too, restricted in scope, providing mainly for those who for one reason or another have no right to insurance benefit.

First for the main features of the unemployment insurance scheme. The majority of wage

[1] By the unemployment insurance scheme is meant the general scheme. There is a separate scheme for agricultural workers with a separate Fund and lower rates of contribution and benefit than the general scheme.

earners under sixty-five years old are compelled to be members of this scheme, though better-paid non-manual workers and certain industrial groups that are only very slightly susceptible to unemployment are excluded from it. Membership involves the payment of contributions into the Unemployment Fund in respect of every week of employment. These weekly contributions, which take the form of stamps stuck onto the Unemployment Book, are payable by the worker and by his employer, and in addition a "contribution" is made by the State. At the present time it happens that the contributions from each of the three parties are equal, and are at the following rates for different classes of persons:

TABLE 1A

Class	*Weekly rate of contribution from each party* d.
Man	9
Woman	8
Young man, aged 18, 19 or 20	8
Young woman, aged 18, 19 or 20	7
Boy, aged 16 or 17	5
Girl, aged 16 or 17	4½
Boy, aged 14 or 15	2
Girl, aged 14 or 15	2

When an insured person is unemployed, then, if he satisfies certain conditions relating to his "capability of, and availability for, work", and if he has thirty contributions to his credit during the last two years, he will receive unemployment benefit. The amount of benefit he will get will depend upon whether or not he has a dependent wife (or husband) and upon the number of his dependent children; but otherwise it will be fixed. Rates of benefit are as follows:

TABLE 1B

Class	*Weekly rate of unemployment benefit* *s.*	*d.*
Man	17	0
Woman	15	0
Young man, aged 18, 19 or 20	14	0
Young woman aged 18, 19 or 20	12	0
Boy, aged 16 or 17	9	0
Girl, aged 16 or 17	7	6
Boy, aged 14 or 15	6	0
Girl, aged 14 or 15	5	0
Adult dependant	10	0
Dependent child	3	0

Although the Ministry of Labour is responsible for the administration of unemployment insurance, the duty of suggesting what changes should be made in rates of benefit and contribution, and also in other conditions, is in the hands of an independent committee called the Unemployment Insurance Statutory Committee. The primary duty of this Committee is to determine whether or not, in its view, the Unemployment Fund is accumulating a surplus, or running into debt; but it has the equally important duty of suggesting how that surplus should be spent or the deficit made good. The Minister of Labour is under no obligation to accept the Committee's proposals; but, as will be seen, he is liable to do so in fact.

The insured person cannot go on drawing benefit indefinitely. If he has not got a particularly good employment record—that is if there are not a large number of contributions to his credit—he will exhaust his insurance rights after he has been drawing benefit for twenty-six weeks,[1] and will have to make application to the Unemployment Assistance Board.

From the applicant's point of view the most obvious difference between being on unemployment insurance and on the U.A.B. is that in the former case he receives benefit at a fixed rate as by right, and that in the latter case his allowance is more closely adapted to his own individual needs, and he is subject to the household means test. The U.A.B. is equipped with definite scale rates. These scale rates, which do not represent applicants' actual allowances, are as follows:

[1] See p. 16, footnote.

TABLE 1c

Class	*U.A.B.* *Weekly scale rate* [1] s.	d.
Householder and wife (or husband)	26	0
Householder, male	17	0
Householder, female	16	0
Other members of household:		
Male	11	0
Female	10	0
Male or Female, 16–21	9	0
Children:		
Between 14 and 16	6	6
Between 11 and 14	5	0
Between 8 and 11	4	6
Between 5 and 8	4	0
Under 5	3	6
Only child (minimum)—if not more than two adults in household	4	6
Lodgers or boarders, male or female	16	6

The scale rates are more elaborate than the insurance benefit rates, since they discriminate between householders and others, and vary the rate for a dependent child with its age.

The actual allowance may be reduced under the household means test in accordance with the resources possessed by the applicant himself and by the members of his household. It is also liable to be adjusted according to the actual rent that the applicant pays; and allowances may be increased if needs of a special character are shown to exist in any household.

The Board relieves the need of those who have

[1] As amended December 1939.

exhausted their right to unemployment insurance benefit owing to prolonged unemployment, but it is also concerned with certain other classes of unemployed. In the first place the scope of the Board is slightly wider than the scope of the insurance scheme, so that certain of the Board's applicants are never eligible for insurance benefit however good their employment record. Then the Board is also concerned to relieve the need of those in receipt of insurance benefit. This last function would be unnecessary if in fact, in the Board's view, applicants were always adequately provided for by insurance benefit. But owing to the low level of insurance benefit, to the fact that benefit is very often not payable for the first three days of unemployment (the waiting period), and to the disallowances that are liable to occur for one reason or another, the Board is to some degree concerned with what are primarily insurance-scheme applicants.

The plan of the book is as follows:

There is first of all a detailed discussion of the advantages and disadvantages of maintaining the dual system of insurance and assistance. If this dual system should be scrapped, and a single service substituted for it, then there would be no sense in discussing the existing services in detail, and in making particular proposals for reform. The chapter includes a consideration of the contributory method of financing unemployment insurance. It is concluded that the dual system should be preserved.

The next chapter discusses the standard of living of the unemployed and shows that this most urgently requires raising. Chapter 4 considers the general opposition that will have to be countered, both through argument and action, if the standard of living of the unemployed is to be raised. Chapters 5 and 6 deal with the scopes of the unemployment insurance scheme and the U.A.B.—that is with the questions of whom these services cover—and make proposals for extension; and Chapter 7, on the relationship of the U.A.B. to other social services, deals in part with another question of scope—that is, which social services should be concerned with which types of needs. Chapter 8 deals with the experience, achievements and limitations of the Unemployment Insurance Statutory Committee, and pays particular attention to its attitude to further increases in benefit rates; it is also concerned with the Unemployment Fund debt. Chapter 9 discusses the raising of child dependants' benefit rates as the most effective method of raising the standard of living of the unemployed. Chapters 10 and 11 are both concerned with the position of women on unemployment insurance: the former chapter discusses the level of women's contribution and benefit rates relative to men's, and the latter the special Anomalies Order that penalises married women as a class. Chapter 12 deals with the waiting period of three days on unemployment insurance.

The next three chapters are all concerned with the Unemployment Assistance Board. In Chapter 13 on the means test it is suggested that the household means test should be abolished and that an innocuous personal means test should be substituted for it, and the present treatment of household resources is discussed in detail; in Chapter 14 the question of supplementation of insurance benefit by the U.A.B. is discussed; and in Chapter 15 the conditions under which additional allowances are granted in winter are examined.

Chapter 16 is concerned with forecasting the changes that would be made in the unemployment insurance scheme and the U.A.B. under the present Government in time of trade depression, and also with the very important question of how unemployment policy and expenditure *should* be co-ordinated with general financial policy, in order that such expenditure should itself have the most favourable possible effect on the volume of unemployment.

Four subjects are relegated to appendices as no proposals emerge directly from the discussions of them. Appendix 1 makes a comparison of average payments of insurance benefit with average U.A.B. allowances, in order to find out whether particular applicants are in general worse or better off on the U.A.B. than on insurance. Appendix 2 deals with short-time working and the unemployment insurance continuity rule; in Appendix 3 the Board's duty to relieve the needs of those who are temporarily disqualified from insurance benefit is discussed; and in Appendix 4 there is a statistical comparison between the applicants to the two services, in terms of the length of their periods of unemployment, their age and the industry in which they are employed.

CHAPTER 2

THE DUAL SYSTEM

IT is necessary to decide at the outset whether or not the dual system of unemployment insurance and unemployment assistance should be maintained under a Labour Government. The first question is, how did such a dual system come into being?

Unemployment insurance was introduced for a few trades in 1911 and made general in 1920. This service, standing alone, was found to be inadequate for the purpose of maintaining all the unemployed in the following three ways: 1. It made no provision for long-period unemployment. If an applicant was unemployed for longer than a limited period he exhausted his insurance rights. 2. Its scope was necessarily limited to those working under a contract of employment, as otherwise contributions would not have been forthcoming from both workers and employers, and it was in practice otherwise restricted. 3. Benefits were at a fixed rate and were often hopelessly inadequate as compared with needs.

In practice the number of applicants who exhausted their right to insurance benefit was so large that very early in the history of the scheme temporary arrangements had to be made for their maintenance. In 1921 so-called "uncovenanted" benefit was introduced, and this was later replaced first by "extended", then by "transitional benefit", and lastly by "transitional payments". Between 1924 and 1925, and after 1930,[1] the unemployed person had a right to this benefit; and at other times it was only payable at the discretion of the Minister, despite the fact that it was not until 1930 that the Exchequer, and not the Unemployment Fund, was responsible for the finance.

These temporary arrangements survived the Great Depression and the first attempt to deal with the problem of long-period unemployment in a permanent manner was made under the 1934 Unemployment Act by the establishment of the Unemployment Assistance Board. The Board might have filled all the gaps in the

[1] A Labour Government was, in both cases, responsible for the legislation.

insurance scheme: had its scope been widened to include all those who were unemployed whether or not they were working under a contract of employment, and had its scale rates been at a higher level, it would have done so. But it did contrive to catch (or to be in a position to catch) most of those who fell right through the net of the insurance scheme, or who were inadequately provided for under it. It made complete provision for the long-period unemployed by paying allowances for the whole period of their unemployment to those who had exhausted their insurance rights; [1] its scope was the same as the contributory pensions scheme—that is, wider than the unemployment insurance scheme; and allowances varied to some degree with the particular needs of the applicant, though this involved a means test. Moreover, it was made responsible for meeting the needs of *all* the insurable unemployed, not only those who had exhausted their insurance rights, and consequently was in a position to pay supplementary allowances to those in receipt of insurance benefit if they were in need. The Exchequer was made entirely responsible for

[1] Except very rarely when applicants were "de-scoped" owing to long-period unemployment (see p. 76, footnote).

the finance.[1] The applicant had no *right* to assistance, but in place of this was the Board's *obligation* to relieve need arising out of unemployment.[2]

In the Minority Report of the Royal Commission on Unemployment Insurance (1932) [3] it was argued that it was impossible to distinguish between two types of unemployed persons—the type for which insurance is an appropriate remedy and the type for which it is not—because whatever classification was adopted it would always be found that "the unemployed are grouped most thickly about a central or normal position".[4] "There is no reason", it was stated, "for the imposition of a means test at the end of a specified period." Consequently the Minority proposed a single scheme to provide for the unemployed. This scheme was to have no means test associated with it; benefit was to be payable for an unlimited period; the cost was to be largely borne by the Exchequer, though

[1] Except that local authorities contributed 60% of the estimated cost of those transferred from public assistance on the second appointed day.

[2] But this is not to say that the obligation to relieve needs leads to the actual satisfaction of these needs (see Chap. 3).

[3] Subsequently referred to as *the* Minority Report and *the* Royal Commission.

[4] *Report of Royal Commission*, p. 392.

small contributions would be exacted from wage earners and employers; and it was to be inclusive of all occupations.

Since the Minority made their proposals the situation has changed a great deal. To them the dual system meant unemployment insurance and transitional payments; to-day it means unemployment insurance and unemployment assistance. To pass from unemployment insurance to transitional payments was a definite degradation—a worsening of status: application was made to the employment exchange, not the P.A.C., but allowances were determined and cases visited on the same lines as out-relief cases, and payments were very likely to be reduced under the means test. Under the dual system as we know it the applicant on exhausting his benefit rights has no connection at all with public assistance cases; he continues to draw his allowance from the employment exchange; and, although he is still subject to a means test, he may very well receive a standard allowance which is larger than the benefit he had been getting, or have his individual allowance increased through the existence of special circumstances.[1] The unemployed are

[1] See p. 187.

still divided up into two groups, but the U.A.B. group is not regarded as less deserving than the insurance group, so that the arbitrariness of the division, on which the Minority justly laid so much weight, need not be taken so seriously. This is important because, if it is difficult to justify dividing the unemployed up into two groups according to the length of their periods of unemployment, it is still more difficult to justify a division which experience has shown does not follow even this rule closely. The U.A.B. deals with an assorted collection of applicants. They are all, except the supplementation cases, ineligible for insurance benefit, but they are not all long-period unemployed.[1]

The only practical alternative to the present system would be a single non-contributory service, the cost of which would be entirely borne by the State. The Minority's proposal to preserve the contributory principle and to derive some income from the contributions of the other two parties would be unsatisfactory, as the scope of the scheme should be much wider than the class from which it is practicable to exact contributions; and the way would have been laid open to increase employers' and

[1] See Appendix 4 for statistics illustrating this.

workers' contributions in the future, as the total State contribution would appear so disproportionately large. The question of the dual system is bound up with the question of the contributory principle: it is impossible to preserve the contributory principle without also preserving a dual system.

Although the precise division of the unemployed is certainly arbitrary, and it is impossible to attach any special significance to the rule restricting the period for which a man can draw insurance benefit to six months,[1] it is nevertheless true that all the long-period unemployed are on the U.A.B. This fact ought to be exploitable. For the needs of an unemployed man increase with the length of time for which he is unemployed and a body such as the U.A.B. (which varies its allowances to some degree with individual circumstances) is far better equipped to meet the special and greater needs of the long-period unemployed than is the insurance scheme.

Needs increase with the length of the period

[1] The period can be extended up to one year if the employment record is particularly good. But under the Unemployment Insurance (Emergency Powers) Act no additional days are to be allowed, and the period for which benefit can be drawn is extended up to thirty weeks.

of unemployment because: (i) Any resources that may have existed at the beginning of a spell tend to get exhausted, either automatically, because unemployment pay [1] is insufficient to meet minimum needs, or through the working of the means test. When resources are exhausted the unemployed man is unable to meet any emergency, even so slight a one as the temporary illness of a child. (ii) Continuous living at the low standard dictated by either of the unemployment services tends to lessen the general resistance of the applicant and of the members of his family. (iii) Long-period unemployment is so depressing that it may in itself lead to physical and psychological ill health. (iv) Household equipment and clothing tend to wear out and need replacement.

Although it is true that those "on the Board" very often get more unemployment pay than they would get were they on unemployment insurance,[2] this is of course not a necessary characteristic of a dual system, but largely a matter of comparative benefit and scale rates. But if a non-contributory system paying flat-rate benefits were in fact to provide for all the

[1] Either insurance benefit or unemployment allowance.
[2] See Appendix 1.

special circumstances which the U.A.B., with its concentration on individual needs, is *able* to take into account, then the level of benefits would have to be very much higher than on the present insurance scheme, and there would be a large increase in the rate of unemployment expenditure per applicant. Were the rate of unemployment to be as low as in 1939, a Labour Government might be able to "afford"[1] the enormous increased expenditure involved in the simultaneous taking over of the whole cost of the unemployment services and the raising of the level of benefit. But this is unlikely to be practical politics in the first few years of a Labour Government's term of office unless there are far-reaching changes in the taxation system. There is a further consideration: although we think that the degree of overlap of benefits and allowances on wages—i.e. the extent to which benefits and allowances exceed the wage that was being earned—is not yet so serious as to provide a reason against any increase in unemployment pay,[2] even so, with

[1] This is a relative word. In our opinion certain other extensions of the social services—e.g. raising of national health insurance cash benefits or old age pensions—are more urgent than the raising of unemployment benefit.

[2] See p. 40.

the new level of benefits, this overlap might be very serious indeed in the interim period before the Labour Government had succeeded in raising the wages of the lowest-paid workers or in introducing family allowances. For both these reasons it is necessary to keep (temporarily perhaps) some form of dual system.

But before coming to a final conclusion the advantages and disadvantages of preserving the contributory insurance scheme will be considered; and in this connection much the most important question is that of contributions.

The contributory method of financing social insurance involves contributions from the three parties—the workers, the employers and the State. The common justification in the case of unemployment for this complicated method of finance is that the workers receive the benefits; that the employers derive advantage from a more efficient labour supply and bear an individual responsibility for unemployment; and that the State must stand part of the cost of a disease of modern industry. Therefore the costs should be distributed between the three parties. But these generalisations are of no help in deciding what proportion of the total cost each party should bear. In the case of unemployment insurance each party is at present responsible for one-third of the total; but this was not always true, nor is it the same with the other social insurances. The only rule common to all the social insurances is the equality of workers' and employers' contributions for all male workers. The proportion of the total revenue for which each party is directly responsible must be recognised as arbitrary.

But even if it were the invariable rule for the contributions made by each of the three parties to be equal, there would in fact be arbitrariness in the proportion of the cost actually borne by different employers, because some part of the employers' contribution is very often passed on in the form of lower wages and/or increased prices to the worker. The speed with which the contribution is passed on and the extent to which this is the case varies from industry to industry, from employer to employer, and depends upon many factors, including, in particular, the flexibility of wages, the methods of collective bargaining and the employment record of the industry. But generally speaking it is important to remember that the worker will be responsible for more than one-third of the total.

In so far as the contribution does fall on the employer it is a tax on wages, not a tax on profits; and this may be a serious consideration in times of trade depression.

Contributions are a most unsatisfactory method of taxing the worker, because, as they are levied at a flat rate, they fall much more heavily on the lower-paid than on the higher-paid wage earner. To put it technically: contributions are a highly regressive form of taxation.[1] Thus the worker's contribution to unemployment insurance is 2·5% of a wage of 30*s*., 1·5% of a wage of 50*s*., and ·75% of a wage of 100*s*. But to state the position this way is even perhaps to understate it. For it is not necessarily only twice as difficult for the wage earner to pay contributions when the ratio of contribution to wage is doubled. At the higher wage levels there is a chance that contributions may be an alternative to saving; at the lower wage levels the contribution is often a direct alternative to bread.

This regressiveness is highly objectionable for its own sake, but it also means that there is (and not very far off) a limit to the level to which

[1] This regressiveness is not in a sense so serious as it might be, as contributions are not payable when benefit is being received—i.e. when the average income is lowest of all.

employees' contributions can be raised;[1] and thus to the possible extensions of the social insurances. Were the tax less regressive more revenue could be raised by it.

It may be objected that it is unreasonable to complain about regressiveness when contributions are not in the usual sense taxation, but are paid in respect of a specific and personal risk. But we cannot agree with this view. Contributions are compulsory and are payable whether or not the individual regards himself as having any risk of unemployment; only a minority of the population is exempt from them; and the proportion of total revenue raised by means of them is, as has already been pointed out, entirely arbitrary. The contribution method of raising revenue must be recognised for what it is.

Because the flat-rate contribution is so unsatisfactory there arises the question of whether the rate of contribution might vary with the rate of wage. Such a method of finance has been adopted by certain foreign insurance schemes.

[1] This level must of course always be a matter of judgment. In considering the possibility of raising unemployment insurance contributions the increased contribution of *1s.* from male employees involved in Labour's Pension Plan must not be neglected. Nor should the various voluntary contributions be ignored (see footnote on p. 28).

The Ministry of Labour in their evidence to the Royal Commission did not consider such differentiation of contribution with wage to be "undesirable in principle or unworkable in practice", and thought that if the scheme were being started afresh there would be certain "social advantages" to be derived from it.

There are a number of considerations. If differentiation of contribution with wage were to be introduced, then there would have to be a small number of wage groups, to which individuals would remain allocated for a reasonable period (though provision would have to be made for movement between the wage groups); and it would probably be administratively necessary to relate contributions not to actual earnings but to wage rates, and consequently to take no account, for example, of short-time working. It is the rule with foreign insurance schemes for differentiation of contribution to involve also differentiation of benefit. But this is not essential. Differentiation of contribution without differentiation of benefit would probably be acceptable. For no additional contributions are paid by those eligible to receive additions to their benefit in respect of dependants. If it were not acceptable, and benefits as well as contributions were made to vary with wage,[1] then the increased contributions paid by, or in respect of, the higher-paid workers would have to be sufficient to finance their increased benefit. But if the employers' contribution were to rise with wage there would be a direct, though small, incentive to the employer not to raise wages; and if the State contribution were to do likewise, the State would be giving more support to the better-paid workers. On the whole we think that the whole cost of differentiation would have to be borne by the employee: but then the variation in contribution would have to be so considerable in order to produce a significant variation in benefit that the plan would be impossible. Consequently we think that the only possible plan would be one under which contributions, but not benefits, varied with the wage. Such a plan might not be administratively practicable, though there is on the face of it, no reason to suppose that this would be the case. It would certainly involve a large increase in administrative work, in keeping wage records and distributing stamps of different values; but

[1] This would have the great advantage that there would be a smaller drop than otherwise in the standard of living of the better-paid workers when they were unemployed.

this should not be insuperable. Wage statistics are so lamentably inadequate at the moment that their usefulness might almost be sufficient justification for the scheme.

But there are other considerations to set against the general objections to financing unemployment insurance by means of contributions. First, there is no doubt that the insurance principle is appreciated by the workers. It is very convenient for all concerned to be able to deal automatically and quickly with those applicants who are unemployed from time to time for very short periods; and contributions—whatever other objections there are to them—are an acceptable form of taxation. It is significant, too, that agricultural workers expressed a desire for inclusion in unemployment insurance, although they were already eligible for assistance from the U.A.B.; and voluntary hospital contributory schemes are very popular, although the same treatment would be obtainable free or under nominal rates with a means test.[1] Further, it would seem rather unreasonable to propose the abolition of the unemployment insurance scheme on these general grounds and simultaneously to approve and strengthen the

[1] See P.E.P., *Report on the British Social Services*, p. 160.

contributory method of financing old age pensions by increasing contributions and raising benefits in accordance with Labour's Pension Plan. The State has a special responsibility for unemployment and perhaps it should, therefore, bear a larger proportion of the total cost of unemployment pay than of the total cost of pensions. But this is no reason for abolishing the contributory principle in the one case and for maintaining it in the other; all that is necessary is that the ratio of the State contribution to the contributions from the other two parties should vary as between the social insurances.

Accordingly we conclude that a Labour Government should not abolish the dual system in its first few years of office. In the long run the contributory method of financing the social services requires re-examination, along with many other features of our taxation system. It might be found immediately possible to vary the contribution rate with the wage rate, and thus to remove one of the greatest objections to the contributory method. It must be emphasised that this conclusion is not an expression of approval of the general ideas behind the 1934 Act, nor, in particular, of the household means test.

CHAPTER 3

THE STANDARD OF LIVING OF THE UNEMPLOYED

It is only rarely that an unemployed man receives sufficient from either the unemployment insurance scheme or the Unemployment Assistance Board to meet his minimum needs. The following table brings this out very clearly. The standard with which unemployment benefit and U.A.B. scale rates [1] are compared is the one that was used by the University of Bristol Social Survey,[2] which follows Mr. R. F. George's standard very closely.[3] The standard was chosen as being the most up-to-date and reliable one available, and for no other reason. The necessary price information for its

[1] The scale rates are those which held up to December 1939. Since 1937 prices have risen at least in proportion to the rise in scale rates.

[2] See *The Standard of Living in Bristol*, by H. Tout, University of Bristol Social Survey, 1938.

[3] See R. F. George's article in the *Journal of the Royal Statistical Society*, Part I, 1937.

compilation was collected in Bristol in May and June 1937, and there is no reason to suppose that it was not representative at that date. The standard gives the amount that must be spent by families of varying sizes if their absolute minimum requirements in the way of food, clothes, lighting, cleaning and fuel are to be met. It makes no allowance for rent, since it was regarded as impracticable to set a standard rent for families of varying sizes, and it also, to quote the Bristol Survey, ignores sickness, savings for old age or burial expenses,[1] holidays, recreation, furniture, household equipment, tobacco, drink, newspapers, postage, travelling expenses and insurance stamps. Even though we are considering the unemployed and not the employed wage earner, it can hardly be regarded as a sentimental standard.

For unemployment insurance benefit to be sufficient to meet the needs of families of varying sizes rent must not exceed the sums of money given in Column 3. These sums actually

[1] Though in 1938 premiums for life, burial or endowment insurance were being paid by U.A.B. applicants or their dependants in 76·4% of all cases. Of these applicants 71·4% were paying weekly premiums of 1*s*. or more, and 28·6% 2*s*. or more. The annual amount spent on insurance premiums was about £1,750,000. (Report of U.A.B. for 1938, p. 73.)

TABLE 1D

	Bristol Standard	Insurance Benefit		U.A.B. allowances			
	(1)	*Benefit rates* (2)	*Available for rent* (3)	*Scale rates* (4)	*Available for rent* (5)	*"Normal rent"* (6)	(7)
	s. d.	*s. d.*	*s. d.*	*s. d.*	*s. d.*	*s. d.*	*s. d.*
Man alone	12 9	17 0	4 3	15 0	2 3	5 0	2 9
Woman alone	11 4	15 0	3 8	15 0	3 8	5 0	1 4
Man and wife	20 3	27 0	6 9	24 0	3 9	6 0	2 3
Man and wife and child under 5	24 4	30 0	5 8	28 0	3 8	7 0	3 4
Man and wife and child 5–9	25 6	30 0	4 6	28 0	2 6	7 0	4 6
Man and wife and child 10–13	27 4	30 0	2 8	28 6	1 2	7 1½	5 11½
Man and wife and two children 5–9, 10–13	32 10	33 0	2	32 0	*10**	8 0	8 10
Man and wife and three children 0–4, 5–9, 10–13	37 8	36 0	*1 8**	35 0	*2 8**	8 4½	11 0½

(1) Bristol Standard—minimum weekly expenditure, omitting rent.
(2) Unemployment Insurance Benefit.
(3) (2) minus (1)—sum available out of benefit for rent after minimum needs have been met.
(4) U.A.B. scale rates (including "normal rent").
(5) (4) minus (1)—sum available out of allowance for rent after minimum needs have been met.
(6) U.A.B. "normal rent"—i.e. one-quarter of the scale rate. If rent exceeds this sum it may not be met in full in the allowance, though it is, with very few exceptions, up to at least one-third of the scale rate.

(7) (6) minus (5)—minimum amount by which U.A.B. allowances fall short of minimum needs, except when the rent is less than "normal rent".

* *Negative sums.*

decrease with an increase in family size; and a point is very soon reached where benefit is insufficient to meet needs *even if no rent at all is paid.* But what rents do the unemployed have to pay? As the average rent of U.A.B. applicants is on the average slightly lower than the average rent of applicants for benefit, the following tables[1] tend to underestimate the rents of the unemployed as a class. They show, in con-

TABLE 2

RENTS

(Percentages of total applicants)

	Free to 4/11	*5/- to 9/11*	*10/- to 14/11*	*15/- to 19/11*	*20/- and over*
England and Wales	9·5	57·1	25·1	6·3	2·0
Scotland	30·4	62·4	6·5	0·6	0·1
London	2·8	23·3	40·2	22·9	10·8

TABLE 3

RELATION OF RENT TO SIZE OF HOUSEHOLD

(Percentages of total applicants)

Size of household —persons	*Free to 4/11*	*5/- to 12/5*	*12/6 and over*
Less than 3	18·3	73·6	8·1
3–3½	12·9	74·5	12·6
4–4½	10·3	73·2	16·5
5–5½	8·1	73·1	18·8
6–6½	7·3	72·0	20·7
7–7½	9·5	67·2	23·3
8 and over	4·7	64·3	31·0

[1] Derived respectively from pp. 68 and 70 of the Report of the Board for 1938.

junction with the previous table, that: (i) only in Scotland do more than a very small proportion of applicants for benefit receive sufficient to cover their absolute minimum needs; (ii) that rents increase considerably with an increase in family size, so that the larger families are for two reasons worse off than the smaller ones. There is no doubt at all that unemployment benefit is, in a very large proportion of cases, altogether insufficient to cover needs.[1]

The position as regards the U.A.B. is more complicated because allowances are varied to some degree according to rent. The "normal" rent is regarded as being equal to one-quarter of the total of the scale rates for all members of the household. When the actual rent differs from this an adjustment to the allowance, either upwards or downwards, may be made in accordance with the general recommendations made by the local Advisory Committee. The most usual procedure is for the rent to be allowed in full up to one-third (sometimes three-eighths) of the total scale rates, or alternatively for a specific limit of 3*s*. to be set to the amount by which

[1] No mention is made here of the supplementation of insurance benefit by the U.A.B. (see Chap. 14). But the number of cases is as yet very small.

rent exceeds one-quarter. When rents are high, a large number of factors (including, e.g., the length of the period of unemployment) may be taken into account, and the Advisory Committee's recommendations are not necessarily followed at all closely. The Chief Regional Officer for London reported that in 1936 in accordance with the rent rules of the Advisory Committee 80% of the cases would have had their whole rent covered, but that the rent was fully covered by an additional discretionary allowance in a further 15%, so that in 95% of all the cases the whole rent was actually covered.[1]

Rent has to exceed the figures in Column 6 of Table 1D if any additional rent allowance is to be given. But for the allowance to be sufficient to meet needs in all cases, additional rent allowances would have to be paid wherever the actual rent exceeded the "sum available for rent" in Column 5. But rents are very rarely as low as these figures, as the previous tables have shown, so it is only very exceptionally that needs are met in full, although the gap between the allowance and needs does not necessarily rise with a rise in rent. Column (7) in Table 1D

[1] Report of U.A.B. for 1936, p. 68.

represents the minimum amount by which U.A.B. allowances fell short of minimum needs except where the rent is less than "normal rent", and gives some indication of the sizes of the sums involved. Although it is true that discretionary increases in allowances are often made, this is only when special circumstances or exceptional needs exist—that is, when the Bristol Standard rates would anyway be insufficient to cover minimum needs—so that our general conclusion is unaffected.

It is therefore obvious that an unemployed man who neither possesses resources of his own, nor is financially assisted by some other person, is almost necessarily living in poverty. This is an objective statement of fact. But how many out of the total number of unemployed are, through the generosity of their friends and relations, or through the liquidation of their own hard-earned savings, actually raised up to the subsistence level? For lack of information this question cannot be answered. It is known that the Board's applicants possess very little in the way of resources,[1] but nothing is known about the resources of insurance applicants. The U.A.B. household means test assumes, but does

[1] See pp. 157, 166.

not compel, the pooling of all household resources, and nothing is known about the degree to which actual pooling occurs. A sample of long-period unemployed showed that in November 1936, as many as 30% of them were living below the George "poverty line", and 44% at a mere subsistence level.[1] All that is known is that the proportion of the total number of unemployed living below the poverty line must be very substantial.

As regards unemployment insurance the official attitude to this state of affairs has always been that benefit was never designed to be sufficient to meet the whole needs of the unemployed person, nor, indeed, to be directly related to those needs, but was intended merely as compensation for loss of wages. But in a world where unemployment may be prolonged; where the unemployed can be dependent for periods up to one year on the insurance scheme; where much of the employment is intermittent; and where savings, owing to the lowness of wages, are often non-existent, even at the beginning of a period of unemployment, this is not the kind of unemployment insurance scheme that we want. The purpose for which the insur-

[1] *Men Without Work*, a report made to the Pilgrim Trust, p. 109.

ance scheme was designed is irrelevant: the ultimate aim must be to pay benefits sufficient to ensure that every unemployed person, whether or not he possesses resources, should be above the poverty line.

As for the Board, it is important to remember that it is not only its own applicants who are compelled to live at such a low standard of living, but that because of the household means test the standard of living of the whole household is also brought down to this level. The principle behind the working of the household means test is that the amount that the earning member of a household is allowed to retain is based on his appropriate scale rate—i.e. on his scale rate were he unemployed. Moreover, that part of the earner's income which is not regarded as available for the needs of the unemployed person is referred to, most patronisingly, as the allowance for "personal requirements".

On the question of scale rates it is justifiable to accuse the U.A.B. of conscious hypocrisy. From the manner in which scale rates were discussed in the First Report of the Board it would be thought that allowances were sufficient to meet needs in all except wages stop cases.[1]

[1] See p. 44.

The Board began its discussion by taking refuge in the differences of opinion that were to be found in various official and unofficial surveys on the cost of living, and by concluding (very sensibly) that "there is no absolute criterion or scientific basis of needs".[1] But since it was concerned to draw up a scale for the relief of needs, some criterion had in fact to be adopted, and there was absolutely no discussion at all in the Report of the actual scales that were adopted, nor of the fact that they were below all those arrived at in the different surveys to which previous reference had been made. All that we get are the following sentences—with their judicious mention of luxury:

> The Board did not deem itself to be concerned with scales of assistance so low as to be merely sufficient to support life. Allowances clearly had to be adequate to permit some variety of diet and some command over items which, having formerly been luxuries, are now conventional necessaries.

In fact the Board is only concerned with needs

[1] Report of U.A.B. for 1935, p. 33. In a letter written on behalf of the Prime Minister to the Children's Minimum Council on 19 August 1936, the view was expressed that "any figures which have been put forward hitherto on a scientific basis are not at present accepted as by any means a hard and fast rule as to the amount required to provide an adequate diet".

to the limited extent that its allowances are distributed roughly in proportion to needs, so that the most needy get the largest sums; and it is only accidentally that allowances are sufficient to cover needs.[1] As with the insurance scheme, the position will be most unsatisfactory until allowances are sufficient for maintenance. It would be the duty of a Labour Government to rectify the position.

This failure of the Board to meet needs is the more shocking when the undertakings that were given in the course of the debate on the 1934 Unemployment Bill are taken into account. It was pointed out on behalf of the National Government that the limit of need was not to be confined to the rate of unemployment benefit; that it was the duty of the Board to promote the welfare of the unemployed—"and you cannot promote the welfare of a man unless you take into account his physical requirements";[2] and

[1] Yet in the Report of the Regional Officer for Wales for the year 1938 the following statement is made: "There are certain classes of quite normal needs which some applicants appear to make little or no attempt to meet from their weekly allowances" (p. 150). Even more remarkable is the following quotation: "From the point of view of the community it is reasonable to hold that young people in receipt of public allowances should, as a condition, keep themselves fit in mind and body." (Report of U.A.B. for 1938, p. 50.)

[2] Hansard, 26 February 1934.

that all needs, other than medical needs, would be met. Had these assurances been taken at their face value they would have involved such a great departure from previous standards of assistance that, as was pointed out by Miss Rathbone on behalf of the Children's Minimum Campaign Committee (now the Children's Nutrition Council),[1] many people were wary of them at the time. Perhaps, it was feared, no more was meant than that the "welfare of the unemployed would be duly considered"—"needs" being a term of "very vague connotation".

The Children's Minimum Campaign Committee were emphatic in a deputation to the Minister[2] that the basis of the Board's scale "should be publicly known and capable of being publicly defended by reference to scientific data established in conference with experts", and the Minister in reply signified his general approval and said that he "did not see in fact what other basis the Board could adopt". In Miss Rathbone's view, unless the regulations

[1] Memorandum on the Scale of Needs suitable for adoption by the U.A.B. in assessing assistance to applicants under Part II of the Unemployment Act, 1934. Submitted on behalf of the Children's Minimum Campaign Committee by Eleanor F. Rathbone, July 1934.

[2] Op. cit.

fitted into the "framework of security" created by these assurances the Government would "incur an imputation of deep dishonour", and it would be said that "Parliament and the country were lulled into entrusting vast powers to a small body of persons, then unnamed, on the faith of pledges which that body has failed to redeem".[1]

[1] Op. cit.

CHAPTER 4

RAISING THE STANDARD OF LIVING OF THE UNEMPLOYED

LITTLE mention has yet been made of the very important fact that the current level of wages cannot be ignored in fixing benefit rates and scale rates. For wage rates are in many cases so low that a small proportion of the unemployed already receive more in the form of benefit or allowances than they would receive, or had been receiving, when employed. This problem will be referred to, colloquially, as the "overlap" of benefit (or allowances) on wages.

It is important to be clear as to why we refer to this overlap as a problem at all, for there are two distinct aspects to the question. First, there is the effect that the overlap has on the individual's incentive to find and keep work; second, there is the aspect of unfairness as between applicants. Now the first question does not only begin to arise as the benefit rate approaches the wage rate; it is always present in so far as any increase in the benefit rate tends to reduce the incentive to work, by increasing the relative attractiveness of the alternative. For there are many factors other than benefit rates and wage rates which influence the incentive to work, and the question of whether the benefit rate affects this incentive does not become relevant for the first time when benefit actually approaches wage. We are not therefore up against a new problem just because in a certain number of cases the benefit does actually exceed the wage.

Nor, for other reasons, need this aspect of the problem be taken as seriously as it is by the Unemployment Insurance Statutory Committee or the Unemployment Assistance Board. This is partly because there is no evidence that the class of applicant for whom the overlap is most serious—that is men with more than the average number of dependent children—is also the class that is least anxious to find work. Of course individual cases exist, and are quoted, where there is definite evidence that a man in this class is work-shy, but in general it is the young unmarried men who cause the Board most worry in this respect. Such young men have sometimes never acquired the habit of working; find it easier to amuse themselves when unemployed than the older men; and have not the same need to keep up a position in the family. And a further very important consideration is that there is normally such a large number of involuntary unemployed who desire to take the jobs vacated by any voluntary unemployed, that a small increase in the number of these voluntary unemployed, or in the incentive not to work, has no effect at all on the *total* volume of unemployment.

But even if it could be proved that, with the present levels of benefit rates and wage rates, a small rise in benefit rates had no appreciable effect on the incentive to work, the question of unfairness between applicants would still remain. It is most unsatisfactory that a man who works should receive less in wages than an unemployed man receives in benefit: it is impossible to deny this. But there is a tendency to think of this overlap as a sort of artificial unfairness, as compared, for example, with the inequalities arising from differences in wage rates in different occupations or in different firms, and for this reason to regard it as far more serious, though this is an unreasonable view.

What is the present degree of overlap? It costs more to live when employed than when unemployed: for the employed man probably has travelling expenses, has to eat some of his meals away from home, and has to pay 1*s*. 7*d*. per week on insurance stamps. And in addition the unemployed man has greater opportunities of subsidiary earning, and "access to assistance from voluntary and charitable bodies which is denied to the man in regular work".[1] Consequently benefit rates and wage rates are made more comparable if some small sum is deducted from the wage rate. The usual sum that is taken is 4*s*., though this is probably an underestimate.

The table on page 44 shows the extent of the overlap for both the insurance scheme and the U.A.B.

The Unemployment Insurance Statutory Committee can do no more than deplore this position. In the report[2] in which they proposed the raising of child dependants' benefits from 2*s*. to 3*s*. they proposed also that the total benefit to any claimant should not exceed a certain limit, for which they suggested a figure of 41*s*. a week. But this latter proposal was not accepted by the Minister of Labour. In a subsequent Report[3] it was pointed out that the

[1] Report of U.A.B. for 1938, p. 80.
[2] Second Report, October 1935. [3] Report for 1937, p. 24.

TABLE 4

*Benefit * or assistance †*	*Percentage of applicants Males*		*Percentage of applicants Females*	
	Benefit	*Assistance*	*Benefit*	*Assistance*
In excess of or equal to wage rate . . .	·9	1·3	2·4	3·5
Less than 4*s*. below wage rate	2·3	4·9	5·2 ‡	10·9

* The benefit figures are derived from pp. 62 and 63 of the Report of the Unemployment Insurance Statutory Committee for 1937; and the assistance figures from p. 22 of the Report of the U.A.B. for 1937.

† In the case of unemployment assistance, the information is based on the wage which the applicant declares to be his normal wage when applying for an allowance.

‡ Benefit less than 3*s*. below wage rate.

introduction of either a "ceiling" or a "wage stop" would increase the number of cases in which supplementation was claimed from the Board. Apart from this the view was held by the Government that such action was too revolutionary to be taken on the initiative of the Statutory Committee alone.

The U.A.B., on the other hand, is equipped with the wages stop. Under Regulation IV, 1 (2) (*a*), it is provided that except where special circumstances or needs of an exceptional character exist, the allowance shall be so adjusted as to be less than

> the amount which would ordinarily be available for the support of the household out of the earnings of the applicant and of other members of the household whose needs have been included with those of the applicant, if they were following the occupations normally followed by them.

The interpretation of the clause has led to a great deal of difficulty. The appropriate wage is very often not the wage that the applicant was earning in his last job, nor the wage that is commonly earned in his normal occupation—it is something much more subjective and arbitrary than this. It is the wage which, in the opinion of the Board, he would be likely to earn given his age, skill and experience and other personal characteristics. Moreover, there have to be deducted from this so-called normal wage the expenses such as insurance stamps and travelling which are associated with employment as against unemployment. Where there is more than one wage earner in the household it is assumed in calculating the normal earnings of the household that *all* the potential earners are normally at work.

This means that an applicant's allowance is

sometimes reduced merely because his prolonged unemployment is held to have diminished his chances of employment at a reasonable wage. So that the possible bad effect on the general health and outlook of an applicant of prolonged living at the Board's low standard of living results in a further reduction of the allowance. Again, circumstances which are altogether beyond the control of the applicant, such as the fact that his type of skill has been rendered obsolete by changed methods of production, may result in the reduction of the allowance.[1]

Though the number of reductions on account of the wages stop is small—5,700 men and 600 women in December 1937—i.e. about 1% of the total number of applicants—wages statistics show that the number might be very much larger. The Regulation is therefore potentially much more objectionable than in fact. Although every applicant for an allowance is asked to state his normal wage, these figures, which would be a useful form of wages statistics, are not available.

According to one Regional Officer, wages stop cases consist largely of applicants with large families who, in the opinion of the Board, are

[1] See Report of the U.A.B. for 1938, p. 11.

normally employed in unskilled occupations; of those who have some disability which prevents them from earning normal wages; and of those who constantly require some special addition to the normal allowance.[1] In our opinion these are just the applicants whose allowances should not be reduced. For, as has been shown, the gap between the allowance and minimum needs is much the greatest in the case of large families; the applicant who suffers from some disability is likely to have abnormally large needs; and the special needs of those who are already receiving some special additions to their allowances has even been admitted by the Board.

The Regulation is altogether inconsistent with the policy of relieving needs; is arbitrary in its operation; and tends to hit those whose allowances would in any case compare least favourably with their needs. For these reasons it should be abolished. The Board's officials would be glad to see the end of a rule which causes them so much difficulty and for which there is such a small return in the way of reduced allowances. This is not a satisfactory solution to the problem of the overlap of allowances on wages. Further, the manner in which the regulation has been

[1] See Report of the U.A.B. for 1937, p. 106.

interpreted can be looked on as an attempt on the part of the Board to classify applicants according to their degree of availability for employment and to relate their allowances to this classification. This is to regard unemployment as a personal problem; not as the failure of capitalism to provide the jobs.

To return to the question of unemployment insurance. The Unemployment Insurance Statutory Committee has provided information[1] showing that, if the child dependants' benefit rate were raised to 4*s*., the percentage of cases in which, in the case of men, benefit rate plus 4*s*. exceeded the wage, would be raised from 2·3% to 3·1%. For women the corresponding percentage is not given, but as women applicants have so very few dependent children the percentage would not be substantially raised. Judging from these figures, the degree of overlap would not be so serious as to provide a reason against increasing benefit. Unfortunately there are no data available which would enable us to calculate the overlap if the child dependants' benefit rate were raised to 5*s*. or higher. However, once children's benefit had reached the 5*s*.

[1] Report of the Unemployment Insurance Statutory Committee for 1937, p. 62.

level, the next step should be the raising of the rates for adults.

But though there is still scope to increase benefit and scale rates, nevertheless a point will soon be reached where such increases will have to wait on a rise in the wage level, and in particular on increases in the lowest wages. Though something could be done through strengthening and extending minimum wage legislation,[1] much the most effective method of abolishing this overlap would be through the introduction of family allowances.

It is probable, if not certain, that sooner or later a Labour Government would be compelled by the force of circumstances to introduce family allowances. These would be financed either by the State or by the contributory method, for it would be important not to upset existing well-established methods of collective bargaining, particularly as the trade-union movement is at present so definitely opposed to family allowances. It must be emphasised, too, that family allowances would not be a substitute for all other methods of raising wages, but would merely supplement them. On page 115 it is tentatively suggested that part of the surplus that is at

[1] See G. D. H. Cole, *Living Wages* (Fabian Society, 1939).

present accruing to the Unemployment Fund might be used to finance a "third child" family allowance scheme—i.e. a scheme under which allowances were only paid to the third and subsequent children of a family. Such a scheme would, incidentally, be a remarkably efficacious way of reducing poverty. A large proportion of all the poverty in this country is child poverty, and a third child scheme would, to quote the conclusions of the Bristol Survey, abolish, at one stroke, as much as 76% of the child poverty that is found in the population as a whole.[1]

The Unemployment Insurance Statutory Committee does not regard the present level of benefits as satisfactory, as is apparent from the following quotation:

> Looked at as a whole, the existing scale of benefits cannot be regarded as so fully meeting needs as to make it undesirable to raise them further, if and in as far as this can be done without multiplying unduly the evils of over-insurance.[2]

But the quotation suggests that the only obstacle to raising benefits, apart of course from the ability of the Fund to finance the increases, is the so-called "over-insurance", or overlap prob-

[1] *The Standard of Living in Bristol*, p. 40.

[2] Report of the Unemployment Insurance Statutory Committee for 1937, p. 24.

lem. In fact, as will be shown later,[1] the most serious obstacle of all is the fact that the Statutory Committee is no longer willing to bear the responsibility of proposing increased benefit rates.

[1] See p. 104 *et seq.*

CHAPTER 5

THE SCOPE OF UNEMPLOYMENT INSURANCE

The unemployment insurance scheme covers, in general, all persons who are employed under a contract of service or apprenticeship, but there are certain important exceptions. These exceptions fall into two groups. There is the group that is covered by national health insurance and pensions and there is the group that is not. Members of this former group are, in general, eligible for unemployment assistance, but members of the latter group are not, and have only one place of resort—public assistance.

The first group, consisting of persons who are insured under the one service but not under the other, includes: private domestic servants and domestic servants employed in certain residential institutions; female professional nurses; members of H.M. Forces; outworkers; railway employees (conciliation grades); [1] public utility employees; [1] and share fishermen.[2]

The second group consisting of those insured under neither service includes: established civil servants; [1] local government employees; [1] police; teachers; and non-manual workers whose rate of remuneration exceeds £250 per year.

In general the excluded persons are only very slightly susceptible to unemployment; [3] though a notable exception to this is the case of the better-paid non-manual workers. In general, too, the workers' organisations are opposed to inclusion—though the non-manual workers are again an exception. In most cases the employment is secure by its very nature, but the present

[1] These classes are only excepted provided the Minister of Labour certifies that the employment is permanent in character; that the employed person has completed three years' service; and that the other circumstances make it unnecessary that he should be insured for unemployment insurance.

[2] The Statutory Committee had referred to it the question of whether share fishermen should be included in unemployment insurance. It decided against their inclusion, though it hoped that some authority with a wider reference than its own would take up the matter (cf. p. 104 *et seq*). See Report of U.I.S.C. on Share Fishermen in relation to the Unemployment Insurance Scheme, 1936.

[3] This is occasionally because the higher grade worker, who is ineligible for benefit, is degraded rather than sacked, so that it is the lower grade worker who actually suffers the unemployment.

shortage of domestic servants may be a temporary feature if unemployment increases elsewhere and conditions of domestic service improve.

Ought the scope of the scheme to be widened to include some or all of these workers? The position of the excluded non-manual workers will be considered separately, so the question relates to the other groups. On the one hand, is the consideration that it is unreasonable to remove many of the "better risks" from an insurance scheme which is concerned with spreading risks; on the other hand, it would seem unfair to inflict the payment of heavy contributions on those who would never claim benefits, particularly as many excluded workers are content with low wages because of their security of employment.

The Minority of the Royal Commission on Unemployment Insurance were prepared to propose that contributions should be demanded from everyone employed under a contract of service; though these contributions would, under their proposed unemployment scheme, have been extremely small ones. With contributions at their present level this would not be a reasonable proposal. And, as was pointed out in the Minority Report, short of an all-inclusive scheme, "there is no logical solution to the problem of what should be the scope of an unemployment insurance scheme".[1, 2] There is not a strong case for widening the scope of the scheme.

Non-manual workers, working under a contract of employment, whose rates of remuneration exceed £250, are outside the scope of all the social insurances: their position will now be considered. In 1935 the Unemployment Insurance Statutory Committee had referred to them by the Minister of Labour the question of raising the remuneration limit for the insurance of non-manual workers, and at the beginning of 1936 they presented their Report. In this Report the Statutory Committee put forward an absolutely unanswerable case for the raising of the remuneration limit.

The Committee supported their conclusion with two main arguments. First, that the excluded class is in practice an arbitrary one; and second, that it is, as a class, subject to the risk of

[1] Report of Royal Commission, p. 443.

[2] "If there is any part of a social insurance scheme that is more the product of chance and expediency than any other, it is the scope of the membership." C. A. Kulp, *Social Insurance Coordination*, p. 210.

unemployment. On the latter point they were unable to collect much detailed statistical information, but they gave it as their impression that unemployment, when it occurred, was liable to be particularly obstinate in individual cases, thus making some provision against it the more necessary. But the lack of information was no hindrance, for the employees' organisations, including the National Federation of Professional Workers, were almost without exception emphatically in favour of the extension.

The excluded class is arbitrary because (i) the limit is based on a *rate of remuneration* which is in practice measured by hourly earnings. Thus it may easily arise that a man is excluded from insurance because he is paid at the rate of more than 2*s*. per hour for a forty-eight hour week, although his actual earnings are less than £250 per year owing to the irregularity of his employment. As the Committee pointed out, hourly wage rates are sometimes higher *because* employment is spasmodic, so that regular employees with relatively little risk of unemployment are insured and casual workers with a high risk of unemployment uninsured. It is impossible to substitute actual earnings for rate of remuneration as it is necessary to know in advance whether a worker is insurable or not.[1] Further—a different point—as rates of remuneration vary, the same worker will sometimes be insurable and sometimes not, and a small, though permanent, rise in wages may result in the sacrifice of all previous contributions.

The excluded class is also arbitrary because (ii) it involves distinguishing manual from non-manual workers. According to a High Court decision the test is simply whether a man is employed for his head and skill or for the work of his hands, and manual work need involve no high degree of exertion. In practice this distinction works out in the most ridiculous fashion. High Court decisions have put both acrobats and professional footballers into the

[1] Under Section 12 of the 1939 Unemployment Insurance Act the Minister may "in cases where the remuneration is wholly or in part of a varying amount and the rate thereof is accordingly not immediately ascertainable" estimate the rate by reference to:

(*a*) The remuneration of the employee in the same employment during the preceding year; or

(*b*) the remuneration during the preceding year of persons in the same grade of employment and working with the same employer or other employers;

(*c*) if information under (*a*) and (*b*) is not available, any other relevant circumstances.

It appears from this that some attempt is to be made to relate the assumed rate of remuneration to the actual yearly remuneration. Before the Act comes into operation it cannot be anticipated how important this Section will be.

non-manual class. The Minister of Labour (or of Health) has put chauffeurs who clean cars and effect small repairs into the manual labour class, as also linotype operators and watch repairers. On the other hand watch testers and adjusters and piano tuners are non-manual workers.

The Majority Report of the Royal Commission was in principle in favour of raising the remuneration limit (and the Minority was of course in agreement), but as it was felt that the various insurance schemes should as far as possible be co-terminous it was unable to recommend an extension. The Statutory Committee considered this view but was satisfied that there would be no serious administrative difficulty in having different remuneration limits in the different schemes.

Although we believe that the cases for extending unemployment insurance and National Health Insurance are equally strong,[1] and would much prefer the two moves to be made simultaneously, nevertheless we agree with this view. For it would be a move in the right direction.

[1] Except that it may be a move in the wrong direction to extend national health insurance at all, when the ultimate aim is a State medical service available to everyone.

And the scopes of the two schemes do not entirely correspond to-day—there are nearly 20 million persons insured under health insurance and less than 15 million under unemployment insurance. Also it would cost far more to extend national health insurance, as the new class would presumably have an average rate of sickness, though its rate of unemployment would be below the average. Further, as the Statutory Committee pointed out, unemployment insurance rights cannot, like national health insurance rights, be maintained through voluntary insurance, as this would mean "a disastrous selection of bad risks".

We consider, with the Statutory Committee, that the remuneration limit should be raised to £400, though we are not particularly wedded to this precise figure. The figure is below those favoured by most of the employees' organisations, but it is necessary to set against these opinions the fact that for those earning more than £400 the current rates of benefit would be ironically small. For this reason the Statutory Committee considered the desirability of a separate scheme for the new class, with higher rates of contribution and benefit. But the idea was rejected for the simple reason that if it were to have been adopted the arbitrary distinction between manual and non-manual workers would still survive.

The Statutory Committee estimated that roughly 400,000 additional persons would be brought into the scheme and that this would involve additional annual contributions of £800,000 from each of the parties. This figure can be reduced to about £700,000 owing to the reduction in contributions that has occurred since that date. As the rate of unemployment would be lower than that for existing insured persons, the extension would have a favourable effect on the Unemployment Fund.

Although the Labour opposition has not ceased to badger the Minister with questions on the subject, the Government has persistently refused to commit itself or to hold out any prospect of future legislation. The latest peace-time Act—the 1939 Unemployment Insurance Act—would have provided an opportunity to raise the remuneration limit. As this opportunity was missed, it must be concluded that owing (i) to the desire of the Government not to offend the employers, (ii) to the additional Exchequer contribution that would be involved, the Government is opposed to extension.

CHAPTER 6

THE SCOPE OF THE UNEMPLOYMENT ASSISTANCE BOARD

REFERENCE has already been made to the "dual system" of unemployment insurance and unemployment assistance. But the complete system of unemployment services might perhaps be more properly described as a "triple system", for Public Assistance Committees are responsible for the maintenance of a certain number of unemployed who are outside the scope of both the other services. The majority of those relieved by the P.A.C. are not, of course, the so-called "able-bodied unemployed", but are sick, or old, or widowed, or members of the vagrant class.

The Unemployment Assistance Board covers all those between sixteen and sixty-five whose normal occupation is employment in respect of which contributions are payable under the Contributory Pensions Acts (or who would have been in this class were it not for the industrial circumstances of the district in which they reside), so long as they are capable of and available for work and not unemployed owing to a trade dispute. In order that its scope should be as wide as possible, it was defined by reference to contributory pensions rather than unemployment insurance; and, at the end of 1938, there were about 20,000 unemployed "on the Board" who had not been insured against unemployment.

On the first appointed day, 7 January 1935, the U.A.B. took over all those who were on transitional payments. It was not until the second appointed day, 1 April 1937, that the remainder of the unemployed who were within scope were transferred from public assistance, leaving a considerable number of able-bodied unemployed on public assistance.

There was—as the table on facing page shows—very great variation in the proportion of public assistance cases transferred to the Board.

The Ministry of Labour explained this variation as being due to variations in types of applicant as between different areas. It is certain that it was also due to the varying practices of local authorities, some of whom, either from ignor-

TABLE 5

PERCENTAGE OF PUBLIC ASSISTANCE CASES MAKING APPLICATION FOR UNEMPLOYMENT ASSISTANCE ON THE SECOND APPOINTED DAY [1]

	Inside scope of U.A.B.	*Outside scope of U.A.B.*
Great Britain	67	33*
South-West England	33	67† (approx.)
North-West England	70	33†
Scotland	79	21†
Midlands	Not stated in Board's Report	
North-East England	Not stated in Board's Report	
Wales	Not stated in Board's Report	
Barnsley	77	23‡
Coventry	43	57‡
Durham District	65	35§
Edinburgh	68	32§
Glasgow	85	15‖
Haslington	40	60§
Nottingham	49	51‡
Preston and Chorley	80	20§
Sheffield	71	29‡

* From Chairman's Report on U.A.B.
† From Reports of Regional Officers of U.A.B.
‡ From Reports of Public Assistance Committees, or from other information supplied by P.A.C.
§ Given in answer to questions in the House.
‖ Stated in the course of a debate in the House.

ance, misunderstanding, or a belief in bluff,[2] submitted most of their able-bodied unemployed

[1] All the administrative areas for which any information was obtained are included in this table.

[2] There was a lot to be said for bluff. It has been reported to us that one Public Assistance Committee was as astonished by the acceptance by the Board of certain "impossible" applicants as by the rejection of certain other "hopeful" ones.

to the U.A.B., and some of whom pursued a much more discriminating policy. Further, the position was so complicated that different officials would have been certain to vary in their exercise of judgment (for it *was* a matter of judgment); and although the right of appeal always existed, the chairmen of Appeal Tribunals were as puzzled as anyone else. It is observed in the L.C.C. Report [1] that decisions of different chairmen were often inconsistent, but that given the variety of considerations involved "this was perhaps only to be expected." Consequently the degree of variation as between areas was not surprising. But we record the percentages, partly to show how great the variation was, and partly because the Report of the Board for 1937 makes no mention of them. This curious lack of discussion of the problems that arose suggests that the whole matter caused the Board some discomfort, and makes it necessary to go to the local authorities for information.

But much the most serious criticism of the Act is unconnected with its administrative interpretation. It is that large numbers of able-bodied

The Coventry Public Assistance Officer admitted in his report to having referred all cases in which there was "the slightest grounds for claiming unemployment assistance".

[1] Report of Public Assistance Committee for 1937, p. 29.

unemployed are, by the nature of their previous employment, outside scope and are compelled to resort to public assistance.

In introducing the Unemployment Bill the Minister of Labour said that, as regards the question of who should be included in the U.A.B., there had to be an objective frontier "which is not susceptible of more than one administrative interpretation". But, in fact, the Act completely failed to define an objective class because of its reference to the "normal occupation" of the applicant.

Long-period unemployment was only one of a number of reasons why applicants were, and are being, declared to be outside scope. The table on page 66, analysing these reasons, is derived from information supplied by the Public Assistance Officer for the County of Durham. It relates to 590 male applicants and 672 female applicants.

The table shows that of those rejected by the Board, nearly half the males and only 1% of the females had been working in their own business; that nearly half the females and only 1% of the males lost their rights through prolonged unemployment; that 25% of the women had never been in employment of any kind; and that in

TABLE 6

DURHAM COUNTY COUNCIL PUBLIC ASSISTANCE COMMITTEE CLASSIFICATION OF APPLICANTS OUTSIDE SCOPE OF THE U.A.B.

	Males %	*Females* %
(i) Not available for employment although capable of work	1	47
(ii) Own business	46	1
(iii) Persons capable of and available for work who have had no fixed insurable employment for some years but who previously had an insurance record .	22	—
(iv) Not capable of work, according to Board, but fit according to P.A.C. records	10	6
(v) No record of insurable employment (cleaners, non-manual workers over £250, etc.)	9	15
(vi) Never been in employment of any kind	8	25
(vii) Others	4	5
Total	100	100

connection with 10% of the males and 6% of the females there was difference of opinion as between the two authorities on the question of capability of work.

In connection with an applicant's normal occupation there are two questions. First, what is that normal occupation; second, when, if ever, does no normal occupation exist. Many of the local authorities say that they were led by the Government to believe that an applicant would not lose his normal occupation merely by un-

employment (thus becoming chargeable to the P.A.C.), whereas in practice this has not been the case. In the course of the debate on the 1934 Bill it was stated specifically [1] that "the mere length of time a man has been unemployed will not of itself, without a host of other circumstances, put him outside the scope of Part II"; [2] and that "supposing that a man is a coal miner, . . . coal mining remains his normal occupation, and as soon as the pit reopens, whether after three years or five years or ten years, he will go back to it and will again follow his occupation as a coal miner. Unless he takes steps in the interval to divest himself of it, that remains his occupation." Again, it might have been supposed that the expression would have been interpreted in accordance with an Umpire's decision [3] (17963/32), which laid down that prolonged unemployment was not in itself a sufficient indication that an applicant had ceased to be attached to his normal occupation. Further, in a Circular sent out to County Councils and County Borough Councils by the Ministry of Health in July 1934, it was indicated that a

[1] 9 February 1934.
[2] Part II of the Act deals with the U.A.B.
[3] The Umpire is the final authority of appeal.

person could not lose his normal occupation merely by unemployment.

But in practice, as has been said, the situation was quite different, and applicants were declared to be outside scope merely because they had been unemployed for the last five years or more (or even in some cases for a shorter period). If non-insurable employment had been taken up, it was necessary to prove that this was of the nature of a temporary stopgap only.[1]

The experience of the Durham County Public Assistance Committee is interesting in another way. Soon after the second appointed day 269 appeals were submitted to the chairman of the Tribunals, with the result that 51 of them were allowed. As the Public Assistance Officer remained dissatisfied, he got into personal touch with certain of the Board's district officers and informed them that many of the applicants rejected by the Board should be taken over as dependants of persons who were already within the scope of the Act. As a result of the further negotiations that followed this appeal, 164 further persons (not cases) [2] were taken over by

[1] See Report of L.C.C. Public Assistance Committee for 1937.

[2] The number of cases corresponds to the number of applicants for unemployment assistance; the number of persons includes all the applicants' dependants.

the Board. In all 2,428 were transferred and 578 able-bodied unemployed remained with the P.A.C. It is probable that many local authorities have not realised what was possible in this way.

Who are the able-bodied unemployed left on Public Assistance? The classification on page 70 relates to Middlesex.[1]

The table provides further evidence of the large proportion of persons on public assistance who had previously been working on their own account. Many of these men were of the "best type", who, unable to obtain employment in their original occupations, took up something of their own such as market gardening. Having lost their original savings they were then punished for their initiative by being held to have abandoned their normal occupation.

The table on page 71 indicates the effect that the transference had on the number of able-bodied unemployed relieved by public assistance.

It is impossible to derive the total number of applicants, excluding dependants, from this

[1] We are indebted to the Director of Public Assistance, Middlesex County Council, for supplying the information on which the table is based.

TABLE 7

MIDDLESEX COUNTY COUNCIL: ABLE-BODIED PERSONS RECEIVING PUBLIC ASSISTANCE ON ACCOUNT OF UNEMPLOYMENT, MARCH 1939

	Number	% (*approx.*)
In business on own account	187	38
Labourers	62	13
Employed at over £250	57	12
Bookmakers' clerks and bookmakers	20	4
Building workers and foremen	16	3
Domestics	15	3
Commercial travellers	15	3
Motor drivers	12	2
Very poor insurance record over a number of years	12	2
Not resident in England for long enough	8	2
Shop assistants	6	1
Clerks	5	1
Musicians	4	1
Canvassers	4	1
Gardeners and farm labourers	4	1
Male nurses	4	1
Motor and cycle mechanics	4	1
Others	57	12
Total	492	100

classification, as there is no means of determining the number of dependants included in (*e*); and it cannot be estimated. It is shown, as would be expected, that the percentage remaining on relief after the second appointed day varied with the insurance standing of the applicant, and that as many as four-fifths of those

TABLE 8

Persons on Public Assistance. England and Wales

	Type of applicant	March 1937 (pre-second appointed day)		September 1937 (post-second appointed day) *		Applicants in September 1937 as a % of applicants in March 1937
		No. of able-bodied and their dependants	%	No. of able-bodied and their dependants	%	
Insured persons	(a)	45,894	10·2	9,799	4·2	21
Dependants	(b)	91,480	20·3	20,495	8·8	22
Uninsured person holding card E.D. 24	(c)	45,639	10·2	18,425	7·9	40
Dependants	(d)	63,809	14·2	24,465	10·5	38
Other persons	(e)	203,331	45·1	159,687	68·6	79
Total		450,153	100·0	232,871	100·0	52

(*a*) Insured persons who hold card U.I.40 of employment exchange—i.e. who have at some time been in insurable employment.

(*b*) Dependants of (*a*).

(*c*) Not insured but hold card E.D.24 from exchange—i.e. the card given to a non-claimant (i.e. a person who does not make application for benefit or assistance) who is registered at the exchange.

(*d*) Dependants of (*c*).

(*e*) All other persons ordinarily engaged in some regular occupation and their dependants.

* This date is chosen, rather than July 1937, in order to allow sufficient time for all the cases to be transferred.

holding card U.I.40 were declared to be within scope.

We think that the U.A.B. should take over all the able-bodied unemployed who are still being maintained on public assistance. Our reasons for making this suggestion are that:

(1) The applicants who would be taken over are not in a different class in respect of employability and availability from those already on the U.A.B. Our information has shown that a large proportion of them had been working on their own account, and that a further large proportion had normal employment records but poor records of *insurable* employment.

(2) Questions of scope result, as we have seen, in a great deal of administrative bother; lead to arbitrary decisions; and cause inconvenience and delay to the applicant. The change would mean greater administrative tidiness and economy.

(3) The U.A.B. was set up in order that a national standard of assistance should apply to the unemployed, and there is no reason why a small class should be excluded from the benefits of this uniformity.

(4) There is resentment on the part of some applicants at having to resort to the P.A.C.

This should not be exaggerated, as the P.A.C. is losing its "stigma" and there is evidence that applicants are often indifferent as to which service assists them.[1] On the other hand, many applicants dislike having to appear before local committees where that is necessary, preferring the greater formality of the U.A.B.; or fear the powers of the P.A.C. to offer institutional relief, or set test work.

(5) It would reduce the financial strain and the inequality of the burden on local authorities.[2]

Other considerations are that:

(*a*) There is no doubt that the main opposition to this proposal would come from those who object to calling persons who had previously been working on their own account unemployed.[3] Unemployment to many people connotes, specifically, the absence of a contract of service; and if no contract of service had ever existed its absence would have no significance.

[1] See e.g. Report of the L.C.C. P.A.C. for 1937, p. 29.

[2] This is assuming that the local authorities would not be made partly responsible for the additional cost incurred by the State. Under the 1934 Act the local authorities were made responsible for 60% of the average cost of poor relief in respect of the persons transferred on the second appointed day.

[3] As a matter of fact, independent workers are even included in some foreign unemployment *insurance* schemes.

But is this really an objection? It is the condition of the receipt of assistance that an applicant should be capable of, and available for, work. This would naturally apply to the new class of applicant whose members would be assumed, by their application for assistance, to have entered (whether temporarily or permanently) the wage-earning class, and to be available for wage-earning employment of certain types. For example, an applicant who had previously owned a shop would be assumed to be available for employment as a shop assistant, or perhaps as a clerk, but not—and this is important—for hard manual labour. It would be just as easy to test the "availability" of this class as of any other class. It is true that a person who is working in a business on his own account is in a position to decide to go out of business at any particular moment; and will be encouraged to do so by the knowledge that he will be assisted out of State funds. But it must be remembered that the shop-keeper values his security as much as anyone else; that there are very few businesses or occupations which one can enter or leave as the fancy strikes; and that the alternative of giving up business and going into wage-earning employment, with the subsequent risk of unemployment, always had existed. An application to the Board would be equivalent to an admission by the applicant that he had been compelled to do something (namely, enter the wage-earning class) which he might previously have done voluntarily. The objection that it is impossible to distinguish between bankruptcy and unemployment is not an objection at all. It is unnecessary to consider whether an applicant is unemployed, when it is clear that he is unable through lack of employment (whether wage-earning or not) to maintain himself.

(*b*) Were the U.A.B. a service devoid of any form of means test the position would be different, as some of the new applicants, particularly those who had been working on their own account, might possess substantial resources. Our proposed "personal means test"[1] would be necessary and adequate to test need.

(*c*) If, as we suggest is desirable, the scope of unemployment insurance were widened to include those non-manual workers whose rate of remuneration exceeds £250, and possibly other classes, the number of able-bodied on the P.A.C. would be considerably reduced. The smaller the number of persons excluded from

[1] See p. 152.

the U.A.B. the more anomalous exclusion becomes.

(*d*) The complaint is commonly heard from public assistance authorities that they have been left not only with a larger number of the able-bodied unemployed than they had been led to expect, but that the cases remaining are in some sense the most difficult ones. The proportion of persons who are for physical or psychological reasons unable to stick to a job—i.e. the proportion of what may be called "unemployables" —is higher among P.A.C. cases than among unemployment insurance or U.A.B. cases, as a record of insurable employment is a necessary qualification for both the last two services. But the absolute number of such persons is in any case not large. And the U.A.B. could be made as well able to look after itself when dealing with such applicants as are the various public assistance authorities. Any applicants who were considered to be unemployable by reason of physical or mental defects would naturally not become the responsibility of the Board. As it is only rarely that an applicant who has been accepted by the U.A.B. is later passed over to the P.A.C.,[1]

[1] An exception to this is the case of 500 or 600 applicants in the Hebrides who were in 1938 ruled out of scope as a result

this means that the record of insurable employment of U.A.B. applicants is not in all cases "better" than that of all those declared to be outside scope.

(*e*) One of the advantages of a dual system of unemployment services ought to be that those unemployed who are not within the scope of the insurance scheme (and this is to some degree necessarily limited) should be eligible to receive unemployment assistance. There is no reason why the same kind of qualification—namely a previous record of insurable employment—should be required for both services.

(*f*) The U.A.B., working in conjunction with the employment exchanges, is well equipped to test the "availability" of its applicants.[1]

of a special review of their position. Many of these applicants were crofters, and were thus not comparable to the industrial worker, and less than one-quarter of those descoped subsequently claimed and received public assistance. (Report of U.A.B. for 1938, p. 160.)

[1] Its methods of testing "capability" are perhaps inadequate. This question is bound up with the need for more administrative co-operation between the unemployment services and the health services. Even on "availability" some difficulty arises, owing to the principle on which the Employment Exchanges act of offering the most suitable men for vacancies, and thus rarely testing those whose "availability" is doubtful.

CHAPTER 7

THE RELATION OF THE UNEMPLOYMENT ASSISTANCE BOARD TO OTHER SOCIAL SERVICES

THE relation of the U.A.B. to other statutory social services is extremely complicated. The Board is responsible for all the needs of the applicant and his dependants, except for medical needs. The applicant himself is unemployed but his dependants are not, so that although the Board's primary function is to "relieve need arising directly out of unemployment",[1] the "character and extent of the help that is required is not conditioned solely, or even mainly, by the fact of unemployment".[2] This is to say that the Board does not fulfil its function

[1] First Report of U.A.B., p. 67.

[2] Report on Co-operation between the U.A.B., the Local Authority and Voluntary Associations in Liverpool. University Press of Liverpool, 1938. (Published with the concurrence and full approval of the Liverpool Advisory Committee of the Unemployment Assistance Board.) Referred to as: *Unemployment Assistance in Liverpool.*

merely by granting an allowance which is adjusted in size according to the household resources, the number and age of the applicant's dependants and the rent. The allowance has also to take account of special needs (excluding actual medical needs) associated with the illness or prolonged education of a child, or with bad housing or undernourishment—and these are not needs specifically associated with unemployment. Consequently the Board is under an obligation to satisfy certain particular needs which other so-called "functional" services with particular remedial purposes are either compelled or permitted to satisfy, and unless some working arrangement is arrived at between the Board and these other social services serious overlapping must result.

First for the legal position. Public Assistance Committees are forbidden to relieve the needs, other than medcial needs, of persons in receipt of unemployment allowances, except in cases of sudden or urgent necessity.[1] Under Section 53 (2) of the 1934 Act any powers or duties of the local authority relating to medical needs, to burials, to mental or bodily health, or education, are expressly reserved. But in practice the posi-

[1] See Eighth Schedule of 1934 Unemployment Act.

tion is not so clear as this statement of it might suggest.

The general problems that arise are best illustrated by particular examples. The question of free school meals will be considered first. Under the Board's original regulations school meals were not in all cases neglected in fixing the assessment. "In so far as meals were provided at school for children whose pathological condition was such that they might be supposed to require additional nourishment over and above that which the parents were able to provide out of allowances in issue",[1] then they were entirely ignored; but in so far as meals were provided for other children it was stated that this saving "might equitably be reflected in some adjustment of the parents' allowance".[1] Consequently in the latter case, where the number of meals taken by a child or children of the applicant's household exceeded twelve a week, the meals in excess of twelve were generally valued for the purpose of assessment at 1*d*. each. It was rightly emphasised that no question of financial saving entered into the matter, and that this was in any case negligible. In the revised regulations school meals were disregarded entirely in all cases,

[1] Report of U.A.B. for 1935, p. 72.

because, as the Board put it, the position had given rise to "misunderstanding".[1]

But this does not mean that all the children of the Board's applicants get meals in the areas in which they are customarily given to those requiring them. In particular the L.C.C. hold that, as the U.A.B. is responsible for meeting the needs of any family in their care in respect of food, clothing and shelter (to quote from the Care Committee pamphlet), "it is not therefore necessary to grant school dinners in these cases except in special circumstances, e.g. illness or absence of mother, bad management, neglect, etc."[2] This policy is justified by the L.C.C. as not singling out the children of the unemployed from the ordinary school population; but it ignores completely the fact that these children are ordinarily attempting to live below the subsistence level. Fortunately the L.C.C. is not representative of the country as a whole in this respect, but even so a survey made by the Board has shown that of the total number of applicants' children attending school only 24%

[1] Report of U.A.B. for 1936, p. 25.

[2] This fact was first brought to light in a statement submitted by the Children's Nutrition Council to the Executive Committee of the London Labour Party on the provision of school meals under the L.C.C.

received free milk, 5% free food, and 8% free milk and food.[1] The Liverpool Committee considered the position,[2] and recommended further consultation between the Board and the Committee as to the development of the service.

Co-operation between the U.A.B. and local Public Assistance Committees is necessarily very close. The Board has set up a Consultative Committee which deals with the various administrative contacts between itself and the services provided by local authorities and in particular with public assistance. The chief reason for co-operation is the Board's inability to meet medical needs of any kind, so that in so far as these are not provided under national health insurance, the P.A.C. has to be responsible for them. As 28% of the Board's applicants have no panel doctor [3] or any other health insurance rights, and as many of the approved societies of which applicants are members do not provide the necessary additional benefits, application to the P.A.C. is very often necessary. But what exactly are those medical needs that the Board is not permitted to satisfy? How in particular is a line of demarcation to be drawn between

[1] Report of U.A.B. for 1938, p. 20.

[2] *Unemployment Assistance in Liverpool*, pp. 11 and 44.

[3] Report of U.A.B. for 1938, p. 67.

medical drugs and special nourishment? The Board was forced [1] to adopt a classification drawn up by an Advisory Committee set up by the Minister of Health in connection with prescriptions under national health insurance, which, although it provided a "satisfactory basis", made the provision of cod-liver oil the responsibility of the P.A.C., though Virol could be provided by the Board. Similarly, insulin must come from the P.A.C., but the Board's category of extra nourishment includes special foods for a diabetic.

The question of the scope of the Board has already been fully dealt with, and the arbitrariness of many of the decisions relating to whether or not applicants should be transferred from the P.A.C. to the U.A.B. has been indicated. In this respect the relation between the two services certainly requires tidying. Also both bodies are responsible for the occupational training of the unemployed,[2] and in the view of the Liverpool Committee there would be many advantages if the machinery of the Board could be open to the use of public assistance applicants. Another question concerns those appli-

[1] Report of U.A.B. for 1935, p. 68.
[2] *Unemployment Assistance in Liverpool*, p. 16.

cants who are temporarily sick. Under the Board's Occasional Sickness rules an applicant can remain on the Board for a period of less than two complete pay weeks, that is for a period up to nineteen days, until he is transferred either to national health insurance or public assistance. The same does not of course apply to sick dependants, nor is the applicant for unemployment insurance allowed such days of grace. As the Liverpool Committee point out,[1] the period of two pay weeks is somewhat arbitrary, and it is doubtful as to whether or not it should be extended.

Finally there are cases of households receiving both unemployment assistance and outdoor relief, where it is the P.A.C.'s practice to reduce relief by the amount by which allowances exceed the relief scale. There is clearly nothing that the Board can do to remedy such a situation—there is no use in producing a vicious circle by increasing allowances by the amount of the deduction—so that if there cannot be local co-operation to prevent such practices there ought to be amendment of the 1930 Poor Law Act.[2]

Sometimes the U.A.B. is involved in addi-

[1] *Unemployment Assistance in Liverpool*, pp. 15, 47.
[2] Op. cit., pp. 15, 47.

tional expense not because the local authority is failing to exert its powers to the full, but because it has a particularly high standard. Thus in explanation of the relatively large number of grants for exceptional needs in London in 1938, the Regional Officers state that this is partly due to the particularly high standard of child welfare work, necessitating special grants for clothing for the children of applicants.[1]

The Board is faced with a number of general and connected problems. Most difficult of all is the question of whether or not to provide or subsidise services which the local authority fails to provide under its permissive powers. Here is a dilemma. If in fulfilling its function of relieving needs it invariably makes good the gaps in the local authority's services, the backward local authority will be provided with no incentive to provide these services itself, and may even benefit from the existence of unemployment in its area. This is particularly true of certain services in which a high proportion of the beneficiaries are unemployed or dependants of unemployed. For example, in Liverpool in 1937 nearly half the children in receipt of free meals

[1] Report of U.A.B. for 1938, p. 80.

were the children of applicants to the Board.[1] The Board would not, of course, in any case, actually provide the meals, but should it in assessing needs take the absence of provision for them into account? If it does not do so the applicant in a district with better social services will still be better off than the applicant in a district with poorer social services, and there will be nothing in the argument (in which the Board takes a particular pride) that uniform treatment is given to all. And another problem: what should the Board's attitude be when the other forms of social service income coming into the household are reduced because of the existence of the Board's allowance?

The Board has expressed a number of general views on such problems; but these are of little assistance in particular cases. It has been stated [2] that "from the beginning the Board has regarded as one of its important duties a progressive attempt to bring to bear upon a household in need through unemployment all the help that the social services, both statutory and voluntary, can supply". Reference has also been made to the ignorance of the Board's applicants

[1] *Unemployment Assistance in Liverpool*, p. 11.
[2] Report of U.A.B. for 1935, p. 16.

as to the possibility of outside assistance, and advisory committees have been recommended to consider how the development of the outside services in their own area might be fostered.[1] This shows that the Board regards it as its definite duty to inform the applicant of the possibilities of outside assistance, but it does not define the attitude when such possibilities of assistance do not exist. Further, it has been explained that "in so far as the special requirements of an applicant or his dependants can be satisfied by a public authority in the normal exercise of its powers they should be dealt with in that manner".[2]

Although the Board has been so inexplicit, various statements made by politicians show that the Board's scales do assume the existence of a certain minimum of outside assistance. Mr. Kenneth Lindsay has stated in the House of Commons that "if free meals were given by local education authorities to all children below a certain income scale, as has been advocated by various bodies—the Children's Nutrition Council, for instance—the Unemployment Assistance Board would be bound to take it into account,

[1] Report of U.A.B. for 1937, p. 56.
[2] Op. cit., p. 6.

and therefore the families would not be any better off".[1] Again, in a letter written on behalf of Mr. Baldwin (then Prime Minister) to the Children's Minimum Council in August 1936, it was stated in justification of the low level of U.A.B. scale rates that the numerous social services available affected this question, and reference was even made to voluntary social organisations which assisted in "the provision of clothing in necessitous cases".

The Liverpool Committee based its general conclusions on the assumption that unemployment relief, like the services dealing with housing and public health, was a "functional service" that "filled a gap caused by the shrinking of working-class family incomes due to long-term unemployment".[2] Being a functional service, and not what Prof. Simey has described as a "Ministry of Persons",[3] it had the specific functions of "relief" and "rehabilitation", and should not, in the opinion of the Committee, be tempted to undertake wider activities. In their opinion the Board should only undertake duties which were primarily those of another

[1] Hansard, 23 March 1939.
[2] *Unemployment Assistance in Liverpool*, p. 40.
[3] T. S. Simey, *Principles of Social Administration*, p. 97, footnote.

functional authority "with the very greatest reluctance".

Such a conclusion will probably serve as a compromise. But it does not affect the fact that it is really impossible for the Board "to refrain from interfering in any branch of social administration",[1] for it cannot help granting additional allowances for extra nourishment or making special rent allowances to prevent overcrowding. Nor will it serve as a compromise unless the very important assumption of a minimum degree of outside social assistance is taken into account; unless, that is to say, the absence of this minimum is itself regarded as a special circumstance meriting an increased allowance.

[1] Op. cit., p. 98.

CHAPTER 8

THE UNEMPLOYMENT INSURANCE STATUTORY COMMITTEE AND THE UNEMPLOYMENT FUND DEBT

THE Unemployment Insurance Statutory Committee consists of a chairman and either four, five or six other members, of which at least one is a woman. No member of the Committee may be in the House of Commons. The Chairman is appointed directly by the Minister of Labour, and three of the other members are appointed after consultation with employers' organisations, workers' organisations, and the Minister of Labour for Northern Ireland respectively. The present Chairman is Sir William Beveridge, and there are five other members, including two women.

The duties of the Statutory Committee are to "give advice and assistance to the Minister in connection with the discharge of his duties"; to report at least once annually on the financial condition of the Unemployment Fund, including the separate Agricultural Account; to make recommendations for the amendment of the provisions of the Act if in the opinion of the Committee the Fund is "likely to become, and is likely to continue to be, insufficient to discharge its liabilities"; and to estimate the cost of any proposed amendments. The Minister must lay any report produced by the Committee before Parliament together with the draft of an Order, and if he does not accept any of the amendments proposed therein [1] he must substitute in this draft some of his own "which will in his opinion have substantially the same effect on the financial condition of the Unemployment Fund as that estimated by the Report as being the effect of the amendments recommended". It only remains then for each House to approve of the draft Order for the proposals to be given statutory effect. By this means it was hoped to relieve the Minister of Labour of the responsibility of day-to-day care of the Fund, and to remove the unemployed from politics.

The Statutory Committee has wide powers,

[1] He has no power to disagree with the Committee's estimate of the *size* of the disposable surplus. "What the Committee find as surplus or deficiency *is* the surplus or deficiency." Sir William Beveridge, *The Unemployment Insurance Statutory Committee*, Political Pamphlet No. 1.

but there are certain types of proposal it cannot [1] or does not make. For example, as it stated in its Second Report, it has decided that it cannot propose, except as consequential on some larger change, that benefit should be paid to men engaged for work but never set to work, or to men awaiting decision of a workmen's compensation claim, however desirable such changes might be; for the financial consequences of such proposals would be so small that they could not be said to affect appreciably the financial condition of the Fund. It appears from the same report, too, that the Committee has denied itself the power to propose changes in the Anomalies Orders. Further, although it can propose an alteration in the rate of contribution from each party, it cannot propose that the State contribution should be other than one-third of the total.

It is necessary first of all to deal with the highly technical question of how the Statutory Committee determines whether or not there is a disposable surplus—that is, a surplus which is available to be spent and need not be held in reserve. In the First Report reference was

[1] A very long list of "Provisions of Unemployment Insurance Acts of which amendments may be recommended by Committee" is given in the Third Schedule of the 1934 Unemployment Act, but the list is, in practice, shorter.

made to a "standard reserve" which, with benefit and contribution rates at the levels at which they stood at that time, and with a given percentage of the unemployed ranking for benefit, was equal to one half the total loss that would have been incurred in the period December 1930 to August 1933 when unemployment was above the "balancing-point"—i.e. the point at which contribution income would be just sufficient to cover outgoings. This standard reserve of "half the total loss that would be incurred by the Unemployment Fund in the worst depression yet experienced" [1] was only adopted provisionally.

In the Second Report, changes in the percentage ranking for benefit, and in the average weekly cost per claim, necessitated revising the balancing-point percentage from 18·7% to 18·1% and the standard reserve to £16,500,000. The question was whether the average rate of unemployment over the period of the trade cycle would be above or below this balancing-point. In estimating this percentage it was assumed that the amplitude of the trade cycle was eight years; that maximum unemployment would be slightly less than the maximum of the last

[1] Report of the Unemployment Insurance Statutory Committee for 1934, p. 13.

depression, say 21% in place of 22%; and that minimum unemployment would be 15%. With the other years distributed in an imaginary but plausible way between the two extremes[1] the resultant average unemployment rate worked out at 17·7%. On the basis of these assumptions the Committee declared the disposable surplus to be about £1,500,000 a year. The proposal to spend this surplus both in the current year and in succeeding years reduced the balancing-point from 18·1% to 17·7% of unemployment, since expenditure would be increased and contribution income would remain the same, and for the same reason increased the standard reserve to £18,500,000.

In their Third Report for the year 1935 the Committee accepted an estimate supplied by the Economic Advisory Council's Committee on Economic Information that the unemployment rate over the next eight years would average between 16¼% and 16¾%. On the basis of the lower of these two figures the average annual surplus of income over outgoings would be £3,588,000, which sum was available for ex-

[1] The following was the assumed succession of unemployment percentages: 19·8, 16·6, 16·0, 15·0, 16·5, 17·5, 19·0, 21·0.

penditure on benefits. But since drawing up its last Report the Committee had become more optimistic and decided that it was justifiable to assume that the existing reserve of £21,500,000 which had accumulated since the debt had been funded, should be entirely used up in the period 1936 to 1943. This meant that a further £2,700,000—or £6,500,000 in all—was available to be spent in each of the next eight years. Unless benefits were only to be increased temporarily and were to be reduced again after 1943, this method of disposing of the reserve assumed that average unemployment after the end of the eight-year period would be below 16¼%.

At the end of the next year, 1936, the total accumulated balance was about £6,700,000 above expectation. This sum, together with 80% of the prospective net surplus for 1937, amounted to £16,500,000. This non-recurrent surplus was translated into an annual surplus, and when spread over eight years meant that £17,250,000 was available for additional expenditure. To continue to distribute non-recurrent surpluses over a period of years, and at the same time to make "permanent" improvements in benefit, was to assume a further lowering of the "balancing-point" after 1944—that is to say a reduction in unemployment in the next trade-cycle period.

Experience in 1937 was again more favourable than had been anticipated, and there was an unexpected surplus of £7,416,000. This was again distributed over seven and three-quarter years, with the result that the "balancing-point" after 1945 was still further lowered to 15·1%. But the total disposable surplus amounted to more than £1 million annually, for since the date of their last Report the Committee had acquired new powers of debt reduction, which they now proceeded to use. Previously, any sums over and above the statutory annual debt charge of £5 million which had been used for debt reduction would merely have brought the date of complete liquidation nearer and would not have reduced the debt charge. Under the 1938 Act [1] any additional sums applied to debt

[1] It is interesting to notice that the Section of the Act relating to debt reduction was inserted on Sir William Beveridge's personal suggestion. The Report of the Statutory Committee for 1936 urged that additional powers for the reduction of debt should be made available through legislation, but the Bill followed immediately on a personal letter from Sir William Beveridge to the Minister of Labour in which he stated that at two recent meetings of the Statutory Committee it was agreed, although no formal resolutions were passed, that the case for amendment had been greatly strengthened by the course of events. The Committee asked

reduction immediately reduced the debt charge, and, since the rate of debt charge was greater than the rate of interest earned, resulted in an annual recurrent disposable surplus. But how much of the present balance should be used for debt reduction? If the Committee had continued to believe in the original estimate of 16¼% unemployment, then, given their reluctance to use the new borrowing powers given by the 1938 Act, no sum would have been available. As it was the prospects were sufficiently bright to make it appear justifiable to use £20 million of the Fund's balance for debt reduction, and thus to increase the disposable surplus from £1 million to £1,500,000 per year.

In the Sixth, and latest, Report it was proposed that a further £3 million, which had unexpectedly accumulated during 1938, should be applied to debt reduction.

Consequently in the first four years of its existence the Statutory Committee has been responsible for the following improvements: raising of child dependants' benefits from 2*s.* to 3*s.* (1935); reduction of the waiting period from

him to ascertain, therefore, "whether there was any prospect of early legislation. . . ." Thus is pressure applied on a tardy Government. (*Ministry of Labour Gazette*, December 1937, p. 470.)

six to three days (1937); raising of adult dependants' benefit from 9*s*. to 10*s*. (1938); and extension of the benefit period for those with good employment records (1937 and 1938). In addition, employers' and employees' contributions were reduced by 1*d*. (1936).

It has to be concluded from this account that the Statutory Committee has not been very successful in its attempts at forecast, and that for this reason it has been able to announce unexpected surpluses each year.[1] The assumption of an eight-year trade-cycle period has been shown to be unjustified, and with it, though the Committee has not yet accepted this, the technique of distributing a balance that accumulated in a single year over a future eight-year period. If the cycle had followed the course forecast for it in the Second Report the unemployment rate in 1939 would have been 19½%.

There is further the question of the Unemployment Fund Debt. A debt of £115 million was incurred in the period July 1921 to March 1932, and it is estimated that £76 million of it (i.e. approximately two-thirds) represented the

[1] Annual disposable surpluses were raised, too, by the assumption that average unemployment was going to fall over the next trade-cycle period.

accumulation of debt over two years from April 1930, which was the date at which the finance of extended benefit was transferred to the Exchequer, and was thus wholly attributable to insurance benefit. There are no data available to show how much of the remaining one-third was incurred for insurance benefit and how much for some form of extended benefit. "Uncovenanted" and "extended" benefit, and transitional benefit up to April 1930, were all, despite the fact that they were not insurance benefit, financed out of the Unemployment Fund. The following table shows how the debt grew between 1922 and 1931.

TABLE 9

UNEMPLOYMENT FUND DEBT

Date	*£ million*
July 1922	14
End of 1924	7
March 1927	25
March 1930	39
March 1931	74
Sept. 1931	102
March 1932 *	115

* After this date the Exchequer was automatically liable to meet any deficiency in the Fund; and by the end of the year the deficiency grant was £4,223,553.

By the time the Unemployment Act 1934 was passed, the debt had been reduced to about £106 million. In that Act annual debt repayments were fixed at £5 million per year, and the interest rate charged after a lapse of five years was to be $3\frac{1}{8}$%.[1] (These figures were £$5\frac{1}{2}$ million and $3\frac{1}{2}$% in the original draft of the Bill.) The whole debt was to be paid off by 1971. At the end of September 1938, the Committee having made use of its new powers of debt reduction under the 1938 Act, the debt stood at £81,530,000.

There has been widespread opposition, even among Conservatives, to the shouldering of the whole of this debt by present and future insured persons. For the debt is quite clearly and obviously the responsibility of the State. It was incurred during a period when successive Governments had abandoned all interest in the actuarial solvency of the Fund. Since there was no provision for the unemployed outside the insurance scheme, and since it was always hoped that the employment position would improve, a series of temporary arrangements, for dealing with the unemployed who had exhausted their insurance rights, were forced on the insurance scheme by successive Governments. Insured persons were

[1] In their first Report (p. 4) the Statutory Committee expressly disclaimed any responsibility for comment on these arrangements. "The funding terms were approved by Parliament after considerable discussion and before our appointment."

not asked whether they wished to be responsible for the maintenance of the uninsured—that would have been impossible, for the insured had not, until the 1934 Act was passed, any voice at all on the question of how the money they had contributed should be spent;[1] and obligations were placed on the Fund which were beyond the objects for which it was created. Many of the persons who will bear the burden of the debt were not even alive at the time when it was incurred.

The Majority Report of the Royal Commission recommended that the debt should be removed from the ordinary accounts of the Unemployment Fund and transferred to a separate account, and that provision should be made for its amortisation in a definite number of years. But, they stated, "We have formed the definite conclusion that it would not be equitable to call upon employers and workers to contribute, separately, at the same rate as the Exchequer towards the repayment of the debt of

[1] This is a surprising feature of insurance schemes in general, considering that insured persons subscribe such a large proportion of the total revenue. Under the 1934 Act insured persons can get their views heard through representations to the Statutory Committee; also one of the members of the Statutory Committee is appointed after consultation with workers' organisations.

£115,000,000."[1] At the same time it was considered that employers and employees had a certain responsibility, as "had proper measures been taken to maintain the solvency even of a restricted and properly controlled insurance scheme", contributions would have had to be increased or benefits reduced. They recommended, therefore, that two-thirds of the charge for amortisation should be borne by the Exchequer and one-third by the Fund. No attempt was made to justify these precise proportions.

It is the Labour Party's view that the debt should never have been put on the Fund, and that what remains of it ought at once to be taken over by the Exchequer. The more years that elapse before this is done the smaller the gain to the Fund. To cancel the debt to-day would be merely equivalent to accepting the proposals in the Majority Report of the Royal Commission.

As the debt charge is now £4 million annually, the immediate taking over of the debt by the Exchequer would increase the sum available for benefits by this amount. Even if the average rate of unemployment were as high as 16·75%, this sum would be more than sufficient to

[1] Report of Royal Commission on Unemployment Insurance, p. 346.

finance an increase of benefits for all classes by 1*s*. and an addition of 1*s*. to child dependants' benefit rates.[1]

Though the Statutory Committee has been no better at forecasting future unemployment than anyone else, it has in another way been a great success. All the recommendations in its annual reports, except an unimportant one relating to the institution of an upper limit of 41*s*. for benefit, have been accepted by the Minister of Labour. This is not quite so remarkable as might be thought, for there is a technical reason why the Minister is unlikely to disagree with the Statutory Committee and himself propose increased benefit rates. Although the Government have got the right to differ from the Committee, they must, in the Minister's words, "come to the House with proposals having exactly the same financial effect as the Committee's recommendations". To reconcile this necessity for exactness with the necessity for varying benefits and contributions by round sums would usually be very difficult, unless the Minister were to resort to making small variations in the period for which benefit could be drawn, or

[1] See p. 14 of Report of U.I.S.C. for 1935, for table of estimated yearly cost of various changes in the scheme.

unless the more rapid paying off of debt were regarded as a legitimate alternative. The only major proposal that has not been accepted by the Minister was one in favour of raising the remuneration limit for non-manual workers from £250 to £400.[1] As this proposal was not made in an annual report, the Minister was under no obligation to, and did not in fact, explain his opposition to it.

But though the Statutory Committee has been responsible for some major improvements in the insurance scheme, it is unlikely, if things remain as they are, that it will be responsible for many more. For the Committee has found itself a little embarrassed by its own powers, and is reaching the limit of the proposals it feels able to make on its own responsibility. The best illustration of this statement is given by the following quotation, which justified the Committee's decision to decrease contributions rather than to increase benefits:

> Any increase of unemployment benefit rates in general should now be made only after full consideration by Parliament as an act of deliberate social policy and not simply because a decline of unemployment has produced a surplus in the Unemployment Fund.[2]

[1] See p. 55. [2] Report of U.I.S.C. for 1935, p. 21.

Again, it was stated that the introduction of a "ceiling" or "wage stop" into unemployment insurance would raise "issues of social policy which should be dealt with only by full Parliamentary procedure after special enquiry directed to the question";[1] and further, the question of whether or not agricultural benefit should be given to boys and girls under sixteen was not discussed, as the existing position was the result of "a deliberate decision of policy by Parliament", and "should not be changed without a full consideration of the educational and other issues involved".[2]

It is very important to notice what this means. Parliament has relinquished the right of proposing changes in benefit rates to the Statutory Committee, preferring to express its "social policy" in other ways; but the Statutory Committee is reluctant to express the Government's "social policy" for them, and may very soon refuse to do so at all.

But the Committee's helplessness is not all entirely self-imposed: part of it arises from the fact that it is only responsible for one of a whole nexus of social services, and is anxious about the

[1] Report of U.I.S.C. for 1937, p. 24.
[2] Report of U.I.S.C. for 1938, p. 16.

effect that its own proposals will have elsewhere.[1] Sometimes in shelving a problem which touches the other social services the Committee appeals for more information and guidance; sometimes, again, it regards it as an issue of "social policy". Thus, it was stated that

> In general, it appears to us that reasoned judgment as to the proper level of unemployment benefit, for men and women alike, involves a fuller study than has yet been made both of the living conditions of unemployed persons and of the relations between wages, benefit, unemployment assistance and other forms of assistance.[2]

Then, in discussing the level of benefit rates it was stated that "it is appropriate to look at social insurance as a whole, and to compare the statutory provision made for loss of earnings through unemployment with the provision made for loss of earnings through sickness".[3] It was then pointed out that unemployment benefit substantially exceeds sickness benefit, but, in mak-

[1] The Statutory Committee have on at least one occasion been compelled to make proposals which were strictly outside their scope. Thus in their Report on the Draft Unemployment Insurance (Anomalies) (Seasonal Workers) Order, 1935, it was proposed that seasonal workers who were excluded from unemployment benefit should not at the same time be excluded from unemployment assistance.

[2] Report of U.I.S.C. for 1935, p. 28.

[3] Op. cit., p. 20.

ing this observation, the Committee were nervous lest they were trespassing and hastened to add that "This comparison does not imply a judgment that the rates of sickness benefit are too low, in relation to need, and certainly not that they are low in relation to the contributions charged ".[1] Although the Committee would be within its powers in proposing a substantial lengthening of the period for which benefit could be drawn, and although, from the financial aspect, this is a very safe way of disposing of a prospective surplus because the decision can easily be revised later, even so, the Committee would make no such proposal. For it regards the question of what proportion of total unemployment be covered by insurance benefit and what should be dealt with in other ways as a "broad issue of national policy" and adds that "the social advantage of providing for unemployment on the principles of insurance, rather than of relief, must at all times be weighed against the fiscal disadvantage of providing for it by a relatively undesirable form of taxation".[2] Lastly, in considering the relation between benefit and wages, it was emphasised that the "prob-

[1] Report of U.I.S.C. for 1935, p. 21.
[2] Op. cit., p. 16.

lem of dependency" needs to be considered as a whole. "To consider it only in relation to persons who are unemployed leads to an impasse in one direction or another."[1] It is unlikely that the Statutory Committee would feel that it ought to bear the responsibility of proposing any further increase in children's benefit rates if there are no changes in other social services.[2]

The Statutory Committee is a neat and ingenious device for removing the unemployed from politics; but it is at present quite unable to fulfil what ought to be its function. The first necessity is that the Government should formulate its "social policy" in so far as this affects important decisions which the Statutory Committee may have to make. It should say that it is or is not in favour of increasing benefit rates so far as the state of the Unemployment Fund permits, and it should also state its attitude to the question of the overlap of benefit on wages. It should state whether or not in its view the institution of a wage stop would be consistent with the insurance principle, and whether or not it desires that children under sixteen should receive benefit on their own account. If, in

[1] Report of U.I.S.C. for 1937, p. 24.

[2] Now that (December 1939) the U.A.B. has raised its scale rates the Statutory Committee is likely to follow suit.

particular cases, a view had not been stated in advance, then the Statutory Committee should ascertain the position from the Government when the question arose. If the Government were to formulate its views it would not mean that it was dictating policy. A Labour Government, unlike the present Government, would have a consistent social policy, and would be able to state its views on these and similar questions. In this way one series of deadlocks would be resolved.

The questions involving the relations between the various social services could not be dealt with in this simple manner. For in many cases legislation, not mere statement, would be required. In some cases the Government might, as it were, tell the Statutory Committee to go ahead, and to ignore the anomalies produced in other places by its own proposals. But this would seldom be satisfactory. Usually it would be necessary for the Government to take concrete action by way of introducing legislation relating to the other social services and to minimum wages and family allowances; and such action would in fact be taken by a Labour Government in the ordinary course of affairs.

The Statutory Committee would still have its

definite functions. It would be responsible for declaring the size of the surplus; for judging how that surplus had best be spent so as to have the most favourable effect on employment; and for deciding how to dispose of that surplus with reference to the needs of the unemployed. In the past the Statutory Committee has tended to be interested in the following questions in the following order: (1) The state of the Fund; (2) the effect of its proposals on the incentive to work, the relation of the unemployed to those supported by other forms of social service income, etc.; (3) the welfare of the unemployed. Instead, it should concentrate on the first and last of these questions, and should be only incidentally interested in the second; and it should in addition relate its expenditure to general trade-cycle policy.[1]

Even before a Labour Government comes into power the Committee should begin to take matters into its own hands. If, ignoring the external considerations, it bravely proposed the raising of benefit rates, the Government would be faced with three alternatives. It could accept the proposals and ignore the indirect difficulties that followed; it could reject the proposals, in

[1] See Chap. 16.

which case the position would be no worse than it had been before, though public attention would have been drawn to it; or it could accept the proposals, simultaneously making reforms in other places.

Though the Statutory Committee could be made to work very much better, nevertheless similar committees should not be set up to keep an eye on the finances of other social services. At present Parliament is the only body which might be capable of co-ordinating the social services, though it would be assisted by the Statutory Committee. But in practice the Government has not accepted this position, and the Statutory Committee has been reluctant to take over the Government's function. If Parliament finds itself unable to fulfil this co-ordinating function—and this is more than likely—the problems will not be solved by having a whole series of Statutory Committees. But a single committee, covering at the very least all the social insurances, might serve the purpose.

CHAPTER 9

CHILD DEPENDANTS' BENEFIT RATES ON UNEMPLOYMENT INSURANCE

In discussing the standard of living of the unemployed it was established that the families that were in greatest need were the largest ones, and it was made clear that it is child dependants' benefit rates and assistant scale rates that most urgently require increasing. The low level of insurance rates was explained by the Minister of Labour in the course of the debate on the 1934 Bill as resulting from the fact that "The Government has regarded as the appropriate unit of variation the benefit given to the parent". Perhaps the National Government would not hold this view now—certainly child dependants' benefit rates have been raised by 1*s.* since the statement was made—but it is significant that it should ever have been its expressed attitude.

If a man on unemployment insurance has a

child he is given £7 16*s*. per year [1] on which to feed, clothe, warm, house, clean, educate and amuse it. Before 1935 he was only given £5 4*s*. per year,[2] before 1924 only £2 12*s*., and when the unemployment insurance scheme was first introduced there was no dependants' benefit at all. If, on the other hand, the man is lucky enough to have exhausted his right to benefit and to be on the U.A.B., he may receive a slightly larger sum.[3]

The costs of raising child dependants' benefit rates are not at all heavy. To raise these rates on the insurance scheme to the U.A.B. level would be equivalent to an average increase per dependant of about 8*d*. per week. In 1935, at a time when there were about 950,000 applicants for benefit, the Statutory Committee stated that to increase dependants' benefit from 2*s*. to 3*s*. would cost about £1,250,000 per year. Therefore to have raised benefits to the U.A.B. level

[1] Or 3*s*. a week. Compare this with the 10*s*. 6*d*. weekly given to householders taking one child under the evacuation scheme, and the 8*s*. 6*d*. weekly for each child where more than one child is taken.

[2] It is remarkable that the 1934 Act did not succeed in raising child dependants' benefits above the 2*s*. level, for we have heard a great deal about its significance as a piece of social legislation.

[3] Unless, of course, he has his allowance reduced under the means test.

at that time would have cost about £800,000 annually.

Such an increase would make good the discrepancy between the treatment of children on the U.A.B. and on the insurance scheme, but nothing short of an increase in the benefit rate and in the average assistance rate to 5*s*. could be regarded as satisfactory, and such an increase should be made immediately a Labour Government comes into power. At the 1935 level of unemployment this would cost about £2,500,000 per year. Whether or not, in the case of benefit, part of the increase should take the form of differentiating the rate with the age of the child seems at this stage unimportant. Only when the benefit is approximately sufficient to cover the minimum needs of the youngest child need the increase take this form. When the administrative difficulties associated with varying the benefit with age are taken into account, as also the importance of making the granting of unemployment benefit as automatic as possible, it appears that a flat-rate increase in benefit would be most appropriate.

The difficulties in the way of any increase in benefit rates have already been discussed. There has got to be a new attitude to the overlap problem; and by some means or other wages have got to be raised and family allowances introduced. But how are these family allowances to be financed? The following tentative suggestion is perhaps worth considering. It is that part of the surplus that accrues to the Unemployment Fund in the next few years owing to the fall in unemployment [1] should be used to finance the payment of family allowances to all insured persons whether they are in or out of employment.

There are in this country about 10 million children under fifteen years of age. To pay allowances to all of them, and to finance it out of the surplus in the Unemployment Fund, would be quite out of the question. About 1½ million of these children are the third, fourth, fifth, etc., members of their families, the first and second members being below school-leaving age. A family allowance scheme under which allowances are to be paid to this group of children is commonly called a Third Child Scheme. Workers who are insured against unemployment have about 1 million children who would come under a third child scheme, and to pay them allowances at the rate of 3*s*. per week would cost about £8 million per year. Were child depend-

[1] See p. 200.

ants' benefits to be raised (as is to be hoped) to at least 4*s*., allowances at this rate would cost between £10 million and £11 million. The net cost to the Fund would of course be less in both cases, as these figures include the cost of paying allowances to the unemployed, and they are already receiving them.

At first sight the suggestion seems illogical and outrageous. Why should the Unemployment Fund be used to pay benefits to employed instead of unemployed persons? But on second thoughts it is not quite so outrageous after all. The alternatives are either extra speedy debt redemption, to which there are objections, or the reduction of contributions. To pay family allowances to insured persons (and to insured persons only) would be to return the sums contributed by a particular group to members of the same group, and would not be altogether dissimilar to a remission of contributions; also it would compensate those who are habitually employed for the fact that they have in the past been contributing towards what are in effect family allowances for the unemployed members of the insured class, though they have received no family allowances themselves. Of course it would be preferable that there should be a self-contained contributory family allowance scheme or that family allowances should be entirely financed out of taxation—but the National Government would have nothing to do with either of these plans, and here we are not concerned with the reforms that should be made by the Labour Party but with more immediate policy.

CHAPTER 10

WOMEN'S BENEFIT RATES ON UNEMPLOYMENT INSURANCE

THERE is perpetual controversy round the question of whether women's unemployment benefits are too low relative to men's. The present position is that women contribute *8d.* and receive 15*s.* in benefit, the corresponding sums for men being 9*d.* and 17*s.* The Unemployment Insurance Statutory Committee have considered the question on several occasions, and notably in their Report for the year 1935. But it has, in fact, always decided against any change, though Mrs. Stocks, in a Note appended to the Report for 1935, proposed the equalisation of men's and women's contribution and benefit rates, through lowering men's contributions and raising women's benefits.

Put crudely the chief argument of those who would wish to improve the position of women [1]

[1] "Relatively to that of men" is always implied.

is that they "put more into the Fund than they draw out". Though the same is true of men, the ratio of the amount received in benefit to the amount paid in in contributions is very much higher. The following figures illustrating this relate to the year ending 31 March 1936.[1]

	Amount paid in in contributions (*1*)	*Amount paid out in benefit* (*2*)	% (*2*) *of* (*1*)
Males	£50,000,000	£36,000,000	72
Females . . .	£16,000,000	£6,000,000	41

Unfortunately statistics are apparently only available for a single year, but there is every reason to think that for this purpose the year 1936 was representative.[2]

Those who do not find these figures convincing argue in one of two ways. The commonest argument is that it has never been the custom in assessing contribution and benefit rates for any particular group or industry to take the actual amount received in benefits over

[1] The figures are estimates and were given in answer to a question asked in the House of Commons.

[2] It is stated in the Minority Report (p. 479) that in the three years 1929, 1930 and 1931, men (aged 21–64) paid into the Fund in contributions just over $3\frac{1}{2}$ times as much as women and drew out of it in benefit just under 6 times as much.

a certain past period into account,[1] and that actual benefits and contributions are determined independently of such considerations. This being the case, the question is how the actual contribution and benefit rates for women were fixed. Was it decided that a certain rate of benefit was appropriate, and was the rate of contribution then such as to make the ratio of benefit rate to contribution rate equal for the two sexes? It might appear that this was the case, for precise equality of ratio would demand that the women's benefit rate should be 15*s*. 1*d*., and 15*s*. is the nearest round sum to this. But if the ratio of benefit to contribution is calculated for the remaining classes of unemployed, consisting of men and women under twenty-one, it is found that it varies considerably. This suggests that the equality of ratio for men and women is accidental and that in fixing the rates of contribution and benefit other factors were taken into account.

This ratio of benefit rate to contribution rate tends to be lower for women and girls than for

[1] But this is not actually the case, for when the Statutory Committee were discussing the draft Anomalies (Seasonal Workers) Order in 1935, the amount of benefit drawn out of the Fund was compared with the amount paid in in contributions, *and the figures were used in the argument.*

men and boys, and it appears that some such factor as the low level of women's wages is taken into account in fixing their benefits. Since these external factors are admitted, why should not one of them be the rate of unemployment?

Connected with this question is one of the strongest arguments for improving the position of women. It is that on the national health insurance scheme women are charged higher rates of contribution than they otherwise would be *because of their greater liability to sickness.* If they can be penalised for their higher rate of sickness on one insurance scheme, why should they not also gain from their lower rate of unemployment on the other? Further, there is the fact of their penalisation under the Anomalies Order.[1]

The other line of criticism of the main argument relating to the actual amounts that women pay in contributions and receive in benefit, is that as a large part of the total of men's benefits is in respect of dependants it is unreasonable not to take account of this in calculating the ratio of benefit to contribution. It is very rare for a woman to receive an addition to her benefit

[1] See Chap. 11.

in respect of a dependant.[1] The Statutory Committee has argued that it is reasonable to look at the insurance scheme as a whole and "to treat the contributions of women in employment as available . . . to help in securing themselves and their children against economic insecurity, if and when they marry and give up earning".[2] The Committee would therefore have been satisfied with nothing less than a calculation which "credited" some part of the benefits received by men to women contributors. But in answer to this argument it must be said that it is difficult to see why the present generation of insured women should be expected to subscribe towards the dependants' benefit of a large number of wives many of whom have never been in insurable employment. A rough estimate suggests that even if benefit, excluding

[1] This is partly owing to the fact that a woman may only receive dependants' benefit in respect of her husband if he is being wholly or mainly maintained by her on account of physical or mental infirmity; the mere fact of maintenance is not in itself sufficient. (Contrast with this the fact that a man may receive dependants' benefit in respect of his wife even when she is in receipt of national health insurance benefit.) The U.A.B. takes the actual facts of dependency into account and consequently about one fifth of the women applicants in December 1937 had their assessments increased owing to dependants.

[2] Report of U.I.S.C. for 1935, p. 25.

dependants' benefit, is compared with contributions, the ratio would still be higher for males than for females.

In an article in *Economica* (1937) Sir William Beveridge attempted to make the argument against improving the position of women even more refined. He wished to find out whether the differences in degree and kind of men's and women's unemployment were what he called "true sex distinctions" or whether they arose from differences in type of industrial employment. He showed that in the manufacturing industries in which a substantial proportion of the employees are women, there is much less difference between rates of unemployment of men and women than there is in insured industries as a whole. He then argued that this modified the usual case for more lenient treatment of women by the insurance scheme. For the difference in unemployment rates was "largely, though not wholly, due to the nature of the industries in which men and women engage"; and therefore "to some extent, the argument for differentiation of premiums by risk must be one for differentiation between industries rather than between sexes". This argument is ingenious: there is universal opposition to differentiation of contribution by industry, and therefore if only the women's case can be identified with this it will soon be disposed of. It would also, as an argument, be conclusive if it were a question of whether or not women's contributions should be lowered below men's because of their lower rate of unemployment. But this is not the question, for there are already differential rates of contribution and benefit as between the sexes. The argument cannot be held to justify the appropriateness of existing rates of benefit and contribution, and the inappropriateness of all other rates. This is of course the sort of question on which "reasonable men may reasonably come to different conclusions".[1] Nevertheless, when all the facts are known there seems to be a definite case for improving the position of women by either increasing their benefits or lowering their contributions. Nor is it as though organised male workers would be openly opposed to such a change. The T.U.C. in its representations to the Statutory Committee relating to 1937, proposed the reduction of men's contributions by 1*d.* a week and raising of women's benefit by

[1] Report of U.I.S.C. for 1935, p. 27.

2*s*. a week so as to equalise contributions and benefits between men and women.[1]

No definite proposals are made here because these must depend upon the other changes in benefit rates and contribution rates that would be effected under a Labour Government.[2] In fixing the new rates it must be borne in mind that owing to the low level of women's wages contributions are already a heavier tax on women than they are on men, and their "regressiveness" more serious.[3] On the other hand there is a greater degree of overlap of benefit on wages for women than for men;[4] but there should be set against this the fact that from the aspect of incentive to work the precise level of wages and the relation of the benefit level to the wage level is not so important for women, compared with the importance of other factors, as it is for men.

[1] Report of U.I.S.C. for 1937, p. 17.

[2] It was estimated in 1936 that to raise women's benefits from 15*s*. to 16*s*. would cost £645,000 annually. (Report of U.I.S.C. for 1935, p. 31.)

[3] See p. 21.

[4] See p. 44.

CHAPTER 11

THE ANOMALIES (MARRIED WOMEN) ORDER

MARRIED women are, as a class, treated less favourably on the unemployment insurance scheme than the majority of applicants. They do not automatically qualify for benefit by merely satisfying the usual statutory conditions, but have in addition to show an actual employment record since marriage, or that they have reasonable expectations of obtaining insurable employment, or that their chance of obtaining insurable employment has not been reduced by marriage. To state the formal position, the Anomalies (Married Women) Order lays down that:

A married woman who since marriage has had less than fifteen contributions paid in respect of her, or who, if more than six months have elapsed since her marriage, has had less than eight contributions during the three months preceding the beginning of her benefit quarter, is entitled to benefit only if, in addition to satisfying the other requirements of the Act, she can also prove:

(1) that she is normally employed in insurable employment and will normally seek to obtain her livelihood by means of insurable employment, *and*

(2) that having regard to all the circumstances of her case and particularly to her industrial experience and the industrial circumstances of the district in which she resides, *either*

(*a*) she can reasonably expect to obtain insurable employment, *or*

(*b*) her expectation of obtaining insurable employment in her usual occupation is not less than it would otherwise be by reason of the fact that she is married.

It is important to notice that the Order does not apply to a married woman who proves that she has been deserted by or is permanently separated from her husband, or that her husband is incapacitated for work and has been so continuously for at least six weeks, or that he is unemployed and not in receipt of benefit.

This discrimination is commonly justified by

the statement that many women cease to desire insurable employment on marriage, so that if in any particular case a woman has had very little employment since marriage it is necessary for special methods to be applied to find out whether she really wants such employment. But of course such a subjective factor as the desire to find employment is not measurable, so that reference has to be made to something more objective, namely to the applicant's expectation of employment. But the objection to this method, and to any other similar method, is that a woman's desire to find work, and her expectation of doing so, are not directly related, so that, as we shall see, many women are disallowed benefit although they are unemployed entirely involuntarily, and for reasons which are altogether outside their own control. In the Majority Report of the Royal Commission it was stated that married women should "show by their acts, and not merely by expressing a desire or intention, that they are in fact still industrial workers".[1] But a test which relies on the *expectation* of obtaining employment does not accord with this.

[1] Report of Royal Commission on Unemployment Insurance, p. 242.

The Anomalies Act, under which the Married Women Order was made, was passed in 1931, and was primarily an economy measure,[1] which arose, as Mr. Maxton put it at the time, out of the exigencies of the parliamentary situation. Two sets of circumstances were held to justify this economy: (1) The abolition in 1930 of the "genuinely seeking work" clause with the consequent increase in the number of successful applications for benefit. (2) The severe trade depression—the unemployment debt was at this time increasing at the rate of about £1 million per week. In addition, such a measure was recommended in the First Report of the Royal Commission on Unemployment Insurance.[2] Consequently a Bill was introduced, which certainly removed some anomalies, but, as we shall argue, created certain others.[3]

[1] On 30 November 1933 it was stated in the House that when the Regulations had become fully operative the reduction in benefit and transitional payments would be at the rate of about £4 million per year.

[2] First Report of the Royal Commission on Unemployment Insurance, June 1931. Mrs. Rackham was the only Commissioner to differ from the Majority Report on this question.

[3] The Bill covered not only married women, but also seasonal workers, persons who habitually work for less than a full week, and intermittent workers; and there were separate regulations for each of these classes.

Judged by the numbers who have been disallowed under it this section of the Act has been highly successful. Many thousands of married women were disallowed in the first few weeks of its operation; in the period up to April 1933, 205,920 were disallowed; and to-day disallowances average more than 4,000 per month.[1] These figures understate the total, since a number of married women, knowing that they would be disqualified, do not apply for benefit. The figures do not relate, of course, to separate individuals, since the same individual may be disallowed on more than one occasion.

The introduction of the Anomalies Act was bound up with the abolition of the "genuinely seeking work" clause. It was in fact a confession that the ordinary administrative methods of testing genuine unemployment were deficient. As Sir William Beveridge put it,[2] the Anomalies Act reversed the "violent inflation of women's unemployment" that had arisen, but "the lesser inflation of male unemployment

[1] These figures all relate to decisions of Courts of Referees. A small proportion of these decisions are reversed on appeal to the Umpire.

[2] "An Analysis of Unemployment", *Economica*, November 1936.

remained".[1] The Ministry of Labour in their evidence to the Royal Commission showed that between February and October 1931 the number of married unemployed women increased from 129,000 to 239,000 and the number of single unemployed women from 166,000 to 238,000. As this disproportion was not thought to be due to the high rate of unemployment in married women's industries, as compared with single women's industries, nor, apparently, to the discharge of married women in favour of single, it must have been, as they put it, that married women were, for other reasons, claiming more often, and for longer periods, than single women.

But even though the ordinary administrative methods had failed to detect certain cases in which the applicant was not in fact genuinely unemployed, nevertheless these methods were, and still are, relatively efficient. This is shown by two facts. The first is that the Anomalies Act brought about a large reduction in the monthly number of women who were disallowed as not being capable of, or available for, work; so that a considerable number of the women disallowed under the Anomalies Act would have been dis-

[1] The same point has been made by the Ministry of Labour.

allowed for another reason had the Act not been passed. The second is that the number of women who are disallowed benefit as not being capable of, or available for, work is proportionately much larger than the number of men disallowed for the same reason. These women consist of both the married and the unmarried; and their disallowance is unconnected with the Anomalies Order. In March 1939, as many as 1,450 women and only 576 men fell into this category. It is evident that the ordinary administrative methods do already detect the lesser availability of women.

Who are the married women who are disallowed under the Order? It is unfortunately very difficult to answer this question. We know the monthly number of disallowances; but we are given no industrial classification, so that we have no idea at all of the number of women who are disallowed although they were previously employed in industries such as cotton and pottery, in which it is the custom to employ married women. Nor do we know anything about the reasons for disallowance, although it is believed that the majority of them occur under regulation 2*b*—that is, owing to the expectation of obtaining insurable employment having been reduced by marriage. Finally we do not know in what proportion of cases successful application is subsequently made to the U.A.B.,[1] although we do know that it cannot be very large because the total number of married women on the U.A.B. at the end of 1937 was only 11,650.[2] In practice all our information must be derived from isolated Umpires' decisions.

An examination of some of the many decisions relating to the Order shows that it produces a great deal of hardship as well as unfairness as between applicants. The factors that are taken into account in determining the expectation of employment include such general ones as severe industrial depression, and such particular ones as the precise practice of the firm in which the applicant was last employed. The claimant's age may sometimes be relevant. In the cotton industry it is a common practice for preference to be given to old employees, and disallowance may occur if there is no prospect of work in a specific mill. Such cases sometimes hinge on whether there is any prospect of a particular mill re-

[1] After the second appointed day married women who had been disallowed under the Anomalies Order could apply to the Board for assistance.

[2] Report of U.A.B. for 1938, p. 63.

opening, and it has been laid down by the Umpire that the fact of a mill being kept in running order is insufficient evidence that it will reopen.

The treatment of married women under the Anomalies Act was reviewed in both the final reports of the Royal Commission. The Minority were more critical than the Majority and were unable to see how such regulations could be "reconciled with compulsory insurance against unemployment". For, as they put it, "the contingency against which the claimant is insured occurs, and, because depression of trade, or the policy of the employer, affects her prospects adversely, she loses her insurance rights".[1] Why, it may be asked, should a married woman who has paid her contributions, and who has, for reasons outside herself, only remote prospects of obtaining employment, be disallowed, whereas a sixty-four-year-old South Wales miner who has been unemployed for five years continues to draw his allowance? It would be as sensible to penalise applicants because they were old as because they were married.

The problem is capable of administrative

[1] Report of Royal Commission on Unemployment Insurance, p. 472.

solution without the aid of the special penalising provision. But no inclination has been shown to solve it this way through the further use of the ordinary methods available to the employment exchanges, because in the last resort the question has been identified with that of whether married women actually need benefit. The matter appears to be merely one involving the desire of the applicant to find work and her expectations of doing so; but this is to simplify an issue that is actually confused. For it is certain that exceptions would not be made in the case of women who are separated from their husbands, or whose husbands are incapacitated or unemployed, were it not felt that in such cases the women needed the benefit particularly. The Majority Report criticised these exceptions on the grounds that they were "in the nature of a grant of relief owing to the inadequacy of family means".[1] The fact was that the exception was tolerated only because the earning capacity of the husband was one of the factors originally justifying the regulation.

The need of married women is very great, as

[1] Report of Royal Commission on Unemployment Insurance, p. 243. This is an odd way of looking at statutory benefit, which is payable for only a limited period.

they are as a class very susceptible to unemployment. The following tables illustrate this[1]:

TABLE 10

Age	Percentage of unemployed women who are married or widowed *	Percentage of insured women who are married or widowed *
18–20	6	3
21–24	21	12
25–34	55	29
35–44	80	37
45–54	67	40
55–64	52	40
Total	46	22

* From Ministry of Labour Gazette, September 1933, and relating to the end of 1932. The figures are only approximate, as the marital state is not in all cases accurately recorded. More recently similar figures have not been given.

TABLE 11

Age	Percentage of married women and widows who are unemployed,* February 1938	Percentage of unmarried women who are unemployed, May 1938	Percentage of men who are unemployed, February 1938
18–20	27	7·9	8·0
21–24	30	7·4	12·1
25–34	20	6·6	10·8
35–44	20	8·7	12·7
45–54	21	12·0	15·5
55–59	22	18·4	19·0
60–64	26	22·4	22·4

* From the Ministry of Labour's Evidence to the Committee on Spinsters' Pensions.

[1] The relevance of the tables is reduced by the unavoidable inclusion of widows.

There does not seem to be any way in which the Order could be satisfactorily amended in order to disqualify only those women who are not in fact desirous of obtaining employment. Accordingly we think it should be repealed, and we think that were this done there would only be very few women who would slip through the usual administrative net and would claim benefit unjustifiably. Married women should no longer be treated differently from other classes in the "degree of availability" [1] required of them.

[1] See Mrs. Rackham in the First Report of the Royal Commission.

CHAPTER 12

THE WAITING PERIOD IN UNEMPLOYMENT INSURANCE

THE waiting period is the three days at the beginning of a spell of unemployment in respect of which no unemployment benefit is received. It is rather euphemistically named. For although it is true that the applicant who is serving a waiting period has to wait three days (and more) before he receives any benefit at all, he never, in fact, receives benefit in respect of those three days. The waiting period is bound up with what is known as the continuity rule. Under this rule two spells of unemployment which are separated by anything up to twenty weeks [1] are counted as continuous, and there is no waiting period after the first spell. Therefore, if an applicant is never continuously employed for as long as twenty weeks he need never have to serve any waiting days after the

[1] The period was increased from ten to twenty weeks in the 1939 Act.

first time. Any three days of unemployment in six consecutive days, excluding Sundays, are regarded as "continuous"—this being known as the "three-in-six rule". No benefit is payable in respect of days which do not form part of a continuous period of unemployment, nor can such days count towards the waiting period.

In 1937 the length of the waiting period was reduced from six days to three in accordance with a recommendation of the Statutory Committee. It had been six days since 1911, except for two short spells in 1920 and 1924. But its "incidence" has varied with changes in the continuity rules.

The commonest justification for the waiting period has been best expressed by the Ministry of Labour in its evidence to the Royal Commission. The argument is unaffected by the waiting period having then been six days. It was stated that: (1) Applicants may be expected to have resources at the beginning of a period of unemployment; (2) the waiting days provide a period within which the claim for benefit can be examined and assessed.

The best answer to both of these arguments is given by the following table.[1] In drawing it

[1] From Report of U.I.S.C. for 1936, p. 18.

up the assumption was made that if the waiting period were abolished no benefit would be payable until three days of continuous unemployment had been proved. These days of unemployment need not, of course, be actually consecutive. If benefit were to be paid for isolated days it would be necessary to abolish the three-in-six rule.

TABLE 12

Day of claim	*Minimum number of days (including Sunday and day of claim, but excluding pay day) that must elapse before any money can be drawn*		*Maximum number of days' benefit payable on first pay day*	
	3 days' waiting	*No waiting*	*3 days' waiting*	*No waiting*
Monday . .	11	4	6	3
Tuesday .	10	10	5	8
Wednesday .	9	9	4	7
Thursday .	8	8	3	6
Friday . .	7	7	2	5
Saturday .	6	6	1	4

The table shows that at present the unemployed man always has to wait six days and sometimes eleven days before he receives any benefit,[1] and that, despite this, the number of

[1] Always assuming that he has not been unemployed during the last twenty weeks.

days' benefit he then receives never exceeds six. As wages are often very low and have anyway normally been pledged in payment by the end of a period of employment, this is a most unsatisfactory position. The table shows that if the waiting period were abolished, four days at least would always be available for the examination of claims and for the necessary reference to the records at Kew.

The Statutory Committee in their Fifth Report regarded the abolition of the waiting period as undesirable, as "money given at the beginning of a period of unemployment is not as valuable socially as money given at the end when other resources have been exhausted". This argument would be more convincing if those who had exhausted their benefit rights had not got the Board as a line of next resort, that is, if it were in fact a question of money at the beginning of a period of unemployment *or* at the end. It is the sort of argument that results from considering the separate social services in isolation.

During the waiting days application for assistance can be made to the U.A.B., and 186,000 such applications were made in 1938, of which 120,000 were granted. This possibility of assistance does not reduce the strength of the argument for the abolition of the waiting period. Waiting day cases are a very considerable nuisance to the Board, for they have to be dealt with at short notice (thus incidentally making household investigation difficult); and involve personal calls at the Board's offices. As the Board holds the view that waiting days are normally "foreseeable contingencies", against which provision can be made, it is considered that assistance should only be necessary where the preceding spell of employment was short or much subject to broken time; where wages had been low; or where exceptional expenditure had been incurred.[1] In cases where urgent need evidently exists, but where the antecedent circumstances ought not in the Board's opinion to have brought about such a position, resort may be had to the powers in Section 40 (2) (*b*) of the 1934 Act to grant part of the allowance in kind.[1,2] The high proportion of applicants

[1] See Report of U.A.B. for 1938, p. 20.

[2] The Board's powers under this Section of the Act are very wide; and its use of them needs to be watched. In so-called "cases of special difficulty" the allowance may (i) be issued in whole or in part to some member of the applicant's household; (ii) be granted "otherwise than in cash"; (iii) be given only upon condition that the applicant attends at a work centre; (iv) be given on condition that the applicant enters a workhouse. The National Unemployed

(65 %) to whom allowances are granted, despite this stringency, indicates the existence of real need.

The above table refers, as has already been pointed out, to circumstances in which the waiting period is abolished, but in which no benefit is paid until after three days of unemployment have elapsed. As against complete abolition of the waiting period (with consequent abolition of the three-in-six rule) the objection to such a plan is that it would extend the period that would elapse before benefit is payable. It would also provide an incentive to the individual applicant to refuse work on the fourth day when the alternative to wages on one day would be benefit in respect of four days. In so far as this assists the wage earner it is not undesirable: nor, in any case, would it be introducing a new *sort* of abuse. For a similar incentive to remain unemployed rather than to work already exists under the three-in-six rule, as an applicant who has been unemployed for two days in the previous five may on the sixth day be faced with the choice of benefit for three days or wages for one.

Workers' Movement maintains that applicants are not notified of their unconditional right of appeal in all such cases.

We do not suggest complete abolition of the waiting period, with payment in respect of every day of proved unemployment, because it would be administratively impracticable; but we do propose the partial abolition discussed above. Those whose spells of unemployment did not exceed three days would, of course, still be in a position to apply to the Board. The Minister has estimated the cost of abolition, with retention of the three-in-six rule, as £1,500,000.[1]

[1] This was a very tentative estimate made in the House of Commons on 6 June 1939.

CHAPTER 13

THE UNEMPLOYMENT ASSISTANCE BOARD MEANS TEST

To return to the question of the Unemployment Assistance Board. We have already decided that it would be undesirable to go back on the 1934 Act: that we must accept the existence of the dual system of insurance and assistance and attempt to do what we can with it. But the implications of this decision have not yet all been examined; and in particular there has been no consideration of the household means test.

The Labour Party has, of course, been strongly opposed to the household means test since it was first introduced by the National Government in 1931. The reasons for this opposition may be summarised as:

(*a*) It penalises the thrifty.

(*b*) It only takes actual present circumstances into account and assumes that the present income of all members of the household is available for present expenditure.

(*c*) It gives undue weight to the fact, not primarily of relationship, but of living together in the same household.

(*d*) It has a bad effect on the personal relations of members of the household, and may even lead to artificial breaking up of the family.

(*e*) It involves detailed inquiries into the circumstances of the employed as well as the unemployed members of the household.

(*f*) It reduces the value of wages and other income coming in to employed members of the household, and thus the benefit that is derived from obtaining employment.

To consider these reasons for opposition in further detail:

(*a*) There are clearly objections to penalising the man who has succeeded in saving some small sum out of his wages. The knowledge of the fact that savings are taken into account by the Board is enough to deter many employed men whose employment is precarious from making any provision at all for the time when they will be unemployed. It is sometimes suggested that the expansion of the social services has reduced the personal responsibility of wage earners; if this is true at all it is largely the consequence of the household means test. This penalisation of savings is as arbitrary as it is unfair. Had the money been deliberately invested in furniture or used to purchase an industrial assurance policy, it would have been ignored in the assessment.

(*b*) The ability of a person to subscribe to the common household fund is not always measured at all accurately by his present circumstances. Although the household means test does, in some cases, take past debts into account, there are many contracts, made in the past, that cannot possibly be allowed for; and the young sons and daughters of unemployed men who wish to save in order to get married and set up homes of their own are badly penalised, though occasionally extra allowances are made to earning members contemplating marriage. Elderly people wishing to save for their old age are similarly placed.

(*c*) It is quite false to infer the inevitability of close personal relationships, or a high degree of financial dependence, from the fact of living in the same household and of sharing the same table.[1] Middle-class people (who were respon-

[1] See *Incomes, Means Tests and Personal Responsibility*, by P. Ford, 1939. U.A.B. households in different administrative areas are there analysed to show the numbers of members that fall into the three groups "natural family", "outer

sible for framing the legislation) tend to forget that members of the working class are often unable to afford the extra expense involved in living separately, and live together in the same household not from choice but necessity. The household means test thus tends to penalise those who are poor because they are poor. And even in those cases where there is a preference, without any financial element, for living at home, it is an entire misconception of the nature of family or household life, or even of the family as a unit of "mutual responsibility," to assume that the members of the household *ought* to be willing to submit to what is in effect the complete pooling of resources.[1] Although there are

members" and others. The first of these consists of husband, wife and children, and the second of fathers, mothers, grandparents, grandchildren, brothers and sisters. Percentages of household members falling into the first of these groups vary between 84 and 96, and into the second group between 14 and 3.

[1] In *Incomes, Means Tests and Personal Responsibility* (p. 61) Prof. Ford has statistical information relating to cases in which the income of the more distant relatives must be drawn upon to keep the head and his dependants above the poverty line. The presentation of the data assumes complete pooling of income, though this not even the household means test can compel. The data relates to twelve U.A.B. areas and shows that 14% of the heads of the families would be aided by persons not even liable under the Poor Law Act (i.e. not parents, grandparents, husbands, wives or children); and that 54% of the heads were maintained by their sons or daughters, and 16% by their wives.

undoubtedly cases where it is reasonable to expect a father to assist in the maintenance of his adult son, and vice versa, these will be in the minority, and many such fathers and sons will not be living in the same household. Also, as we have seen, all members of the same household are not always members of the same family. An arrangement to live together in the same household is often more arbitrary than a middle-class person might suppose.

(*d*) It is impossible to exaggerate the dislike of the ordinary person who is normally financially independent at being compelled to accept pocket-money from the earning members of his household. Even if the money is given willingly it may only be accepted most reluctantly, or not at all, so that there are two standards of living in the same family. The means test exaggerates the feeling of inferiority that an unemployed member of a household is in any case liable to feel. Probation officers testify to the complete loss of authority suffered by the father when the means test deprives him of any income of his own. The extent to which families have been broken up has probably been exaggerated. In the First Report of the U.A.B. the District Officers referred to the alleged break up of households, and most of them were agreed that the problem was not very important, but that when break up did occur it was very often in those households in which strains had existed previously, the means test supplying the extra incentive for leaving. But, most unfortunately, one reason why the means test has not led to more breaking up of households is because, if the Board suspects that there has been " collusion between the applicant and his parents for the purpose of evading the test of need",[1] the allowances will not be increased.[2]

(*e*) One of the most objectionable features of the household means test is the actual investigation that is involved; and this investigation involves employed and unemployed alike, though the former are absent when the investigator calls.

(*f*) If there is anything in the argument that an increase in benefit would reduce the incentive to work, then the effect of the household means test in reducing the effective wages of the employed members of the household must not be ignored.

[1] Report of U.A.B. for 1935, p. 158.

[2] There is evidence that long-period unemployment leads to unemployed persons taking refuge with other members of the family. See P. Ford, op. cit., p. 36.

The household means test is a direct inheritance from the Poor Law and was not discarded when those already under it on transitional payments were transferred to the Unemployment Assistance Board. Its persistence is an acknowledgment of the fact that unemployment assistance is analogous to relief. There is no doubt at all that the household means test should be abolished.

But this is not to say that the Board could do without any form of means test. It has already been pointed out that one of the chief justifications for the Board's existence is that it is capable of adjusting its allowances to satisfy the extra, and sometimes peculiar, needs of the long-period unemployed. Without a means test of some kind it would be quite impossible to diagnose and to relieve these particular needs, for in order that needs may be assessed, means must first be ascertained. Neither special circumstances nor exceptional needs could be detected were there no means test; and it would be quite unreasonable to give increased allowances in such cases and never to deduct anything from the allowance because of the existence of extra large resources available for the support of the applicant. A means test of some kind is not an incidental but an integral part of the U.A.B.; and if it were to be abolished altogether the U.A.B. in its present form would have to go too.

The question is, how can the necessity for some form of means test which will enable the Board to diagnose the need of the applicant and of his family be reconciled with this strong opposition to the household means test? It will be noticed that all the objections to the household means test that have been examined, except the question of the penalisation of thrift, depended on the fact that it takes the resources of the whole of the applicant's household into account, and were not generalised objections to means tests *per se*. This is not surprising, as a Labour Government would inevitably continue to operate means tests in connection with many of the social services.[1] A satisfactory solution would be to substitute for the household means test what can be called a *personal means test* which would apply to the applicant, to his wife (or husband) and to any other person in respect of whom dependants' benefit is claimed from the Board. Thus would the means test and the needs test be made to correspond.

[1] There are nineteen different services (apart from evacuation) in which means tests may be used. *Incomes, Means Tests and Personal Responsibility*, p. 14.

The fact of the Minority Report's emphatic opposition to any form of means test is not relevant to-day. For, as has already been argued,[1] the situation was entirely different before the U.A.B. existed. There was no possibility then, as there is now, of allowances being increased, consequent (and this is to put it provocatively) on the operation of the means test. But the Minority Report did favour a personal means test for applicants who had been in receipt of wages and who had no employment record, on the grounds that they should "properly be asked to show that they do actually look to wage earning for a livelihood". If there were no means test it would be quite out of the question to expand the scope of the U.A.B. to cover persons who had previously been working on their own account.[2]

Before discussing the details of the personal means test, it is interesting to refer to the Minister of Labour's justification for the Government's household means test, when, in introducing the 1934 Bill, he said: Were there no means test it would "involve the closest control by the State of the terms and conditions of industrial employment" . . . "in its own

[1] See p. 14. [2] See Chap. 6.

interests the State would have to impose strict discipline and control over the private actions of unemployed persons . . . and for its own protection determine what kind of employment the worker should be willing to take and upon what terms". He added that he was satisfied that "the workers themselves would never agree to the regimentation involved in such a policy".

This personal means test should ordinarily take the form of a declaration of personal income by the claimant at the Exchange. The Minority Report sets out a detailed procedure for this [1] which would appear to be appropriate in its broad outline to-day. It is suggested that the applicant should fill in his form at home and should get it witnessed by a responsible person, and that the insurance officer should be in a position to arrange for any statement which appeared to him to be doubtful to be checked by an investigating officer. The existence of doubtful or difficult cases would not, of course, be the only reason for keeping on investigating officers; for it is impossible to exaggerate the importance of the "personal element" in the administration of the Board. But the Board would be expected only to find a small minority of cases so "diffi-

[1] Minority Report of Royal Commission, p. 417.

cult" as to require investigation for this reason alone.[1]

We make this last proposal both for the saving in administrative costs which it would entail and because (more important) of the extent to which the ordinary applicant dislikes having his household resources minutely investigated by the "means test man". To many people the means test is completely identified with the investigating officer. As has been said, much of the original hostility to the household means test was "caused by the method of administration rather than by the idea of the test itself".[2] It is stated in *Men Without Work*[3] that the impression formed by those who took part in the inquiry was that, on the whole, the Board's officers carry out their duty with "tact and sympathy", but that one of the troubles is that "everybody knows who the means test man is when he comes to call on you", and another that there is always fear (however unjustified) that tales of a man's business will "get about". There is naturally

[1] But it would be a mistake to be too optimistic. At the outbreak of war the Board was compelled to give allowances on the basis of statements, but subsequent investigation brought some inaccuracies to light.

[2] *The State and the Standard of Living*, by Gertrude Williams, 1936.

[3] A Report made to the Pilgrim Trust, 1938, p. 438.

much resentment at the questioning intrusion of the officer.[1] There should also be reform of the method of appointment of investigating clerks, who are badly paid [2] and insufficiently skilled.

Next we come to the actual details of the proposed personal means test. The household means test is such a ruthless instrument that it was found necessary, following on the example of public assistance, to "protect" certain resources—i.e. to lay down that the whole or part of the income derived from them should not be taken into account in assessing need. The position is set out in the tables on pages 157 and 166.

[1] In reply to a number of questions in the House on 26 May 1938, the Minister of Labour stated that the following instructions had been issued by the U.A.B. The need for such instructions illustrates the dangers of the investigating officer system. "Reports by investigating officers must be strictly confined to the recording of matters which are relevant to the determination of allowances or to other decisions, e.g. in regard to eligibility for training, which it is competent for officers of the Board to take. The religious or political views of applicants are wholly irrelevant to such decisions, and the greatest care must be taken by officers of all ranks to exclude any comments on such matters from their reports on the circumstances of the applicants and their households."

[2] This is still true despite the small increases that are now to be granted (December 1939). These increases are far smaller than those claimed by the Civil Service Clerical Association (see their illuminating *Statement of Case to the Civil Service Arbitration Tribunal*).

TABLE 13

PROTECTED RESOURCES *

Type of resource	*Amount of weekly income protected*	*Estimated annual value of resources of all U.A.B, applicants in 1937*†	
		Applicant	*Wife (or husband)*
Friendly society sick pay	5*s*.		
National health insurance cash benefit	7*s*. 6*d*.	£8,500	£60,600
National health insurance maternity benefit	First maternity benefit and second in practice ‡		
Wounds or disability pension	£1	£903,600 §	£63,500
Workmen's compensation	½ of weekly payments ‖	£101,300	£2,600
Capital assets	Amounts up to £50	£48,500	£8,600
Reserve pay.	5*s*. ¶	£62,900	—
Trade union unemployment benefit	5*s*.		
School meals and milk.	The whole **		
Educational grants	The whole ††		
War widows' and service dependants' pensions	30*s*.	£76,700	£25,000

* The majority of these resources are statutorily protected; but in some cases the Board has merely issued instructions to its officers, though the distinction is unimportant. The list does not, of course, include all forms of resources.

† From Report of U.A.B. for 1937, p. 190. Where no information is given it means that it is not available from this source.

‡ Additional benefit and second maternity benefit are not statutorily protected; and the former, though not the present, practice, was to disregard such resources only where special needs were shown to exist.

§ These sums include disability and dependants' pensions.

‖ Where weekly payments are commuted for a lump sum, one half of it is treated as a capital asset, and the other half is ignored, i.e. protected.

¶ The additional 6*d*. per day received by a member of Section A of the Army Reserve is also protected.

** Under the original regulations school meals were in certain circumstances taken into account.

†† Except in exceptional cases when amounts are very large.

Practically all the individuals whose resources are protected have special needs resulting from disability, sickness or old age. But is there any association between the degree of sickness, etc. (and thus the needs), and the actual amount of income that is protected? For in deciding what relative amounts of the various forms of income to protect, the only consideration should be the special need with which they are associated.

Although the personal means test would be very mild in its operation compared with the present household means test, and therefore the need to keep it under control would not be so great, nevertheless certain resources should still be protected. This is because: (1) It is often impossible to measure at all accurately the need associated with a given form of income, so that it is better to lay down general rules. (2) Allowances are usually so grossly inadequate [1] that we could not make any proposal which might have the effect of reducing the amount paid to any class of applicant, particularly those with special needs. (3) It is most important not to penalise thriftiness.

We would lay down the following principles: (*a*) That as far as possible all resources should

[1] See p. 29.

be given equal treatment in accordance only with the needs associated with their receipt; (*b*) that no distinction should be made between resources belonging to the applicant and those belonging to the wife (or husband) of the applicant; (*c*) that if incomes from more than one source are being received in respect of the same need (e.g. sickness), protection should not be afforded to each income separately, but only to the total sum.

At present there is insufficient protection; nor is it consistent with the above principles. There is no reason why more protection should be given to national health insurance cash benefits than to friendly society sick pay. The fact that one is a State scheme involving contributions from the usual three parties, and the other is not, is altogether irrelevant. And why are disability pensions given, on the average, more protection than workmen's compensation? There are many other obvious discrepancies.

As regards capital resources, the present position is that the first £25 is disregarded, the next £275 is treated as yielding 1*s*. a week for each complete £25—that is, a rate of 10%; and anything over £300 is regarded as directly available to meet the current needs of the household,[1] so that the applicant is given a nil determination (i.e. a zero allowance) until the sum is reduced to £300. Capital resources include all the usual forms of saving except the house in which the applicant resides.

In considering this question it is important to notice that the income derived by the unemployed person and his wife (or husband) from savings, capital and property [2] is equal to only 2% of the total income derived from all resources, which means that the number of U.A.B. applicants who possess resources of any size at all is extremely small. But, and it is very important to remember this, the table in the U.A.B. Report to which we refer [3] does not include the capital resources of those unemployed persons who are given nil determinations by the Board, and those who do not apply to the Board at all because they anticipate receiving no allowance or are not prepared to subject their relatives to the household means test. The abolition of the

[1] These rules apply to the applicant or his wife, husband, father or mother; for other members of the household the *actual* income is taken into account, and there is an upper limit of £400.

[2] See p. 190 of the Report of U.A.B. for 1937. The estimated annual value of the savings, capital and property is based mainly on the 1*s*. for every £25 rule.

[3] Report of U.A.B. for 1937, p. 190.

household means test would bring some of these unemployed persons on to the Board.[1]

The present rule is most objectionable. As the assumed rate of interest is 10% on each complete £25 after the first £25, and as the actual rate of interest is unlikely to be anything in the neighbourhood of this figure, the rule is extremely likely to result in the enforced expenditure or liquidation of such resources as may exist and will also reduce the incentive of the employed person to save. It is most pernicious that those who have succeeded in saving some small sum out of their wages should be penalised for this, and should be forced to realise their capital at what may be a highly inconvenient moment.

Those who signed the Majority Report of the Royal Commission stated that they found

[1] The number would not be negligible. The Minister of Labour has stated that on 14 March 1938 there were 51,716 men, 38,751 women, 10,263 juveniles aged sixteen and seventeen, and 33,863 under sixteen, on the registers of employment exchanges in Great Britain who had made no application for benefit or unemployment allowances (Hansard, 17 April 1938). On 23 June 1938 it was stated that during the financial year 1937–38, 97,153 nil determinations were made in cases where the applicant was adjudged to be not in need of an allowance. The same individual may be included more than once in this total, and it probably includes a large number of applicants claiming only in respect of the waiting period.

"several difficulties in the way of laying down a general rule for the treatment of savings".[1] However, they actually recommended the rule which found its way into the 1934 Act and which has survived until to-day. But they were afraid of appearing over-generous [2] and wished this rule only to apply to what they called "genuine savings", which were distinct from accumulated earnings or deferred pay. Here again we come across the tendency, which has been observed elsewhere, for the authorities to consider not only needs but deserts. But in this case the Majority do not even examine why the unemployed person whose deferred pay represents his savings is less deserving than the unemployed man whose savings are "genuine" because he inherited them from his uncle. It is difficult to see how there could be any criterion of the "genuineness" of savings.

In the chapter of the Minority Report which dealt with the relief scheme proposed by the Majority it was proposed that the assumed interest rate on capital resources should be 3½%

[1] Report of Royal Commission on Unemployment Insurance, p. 290.

[2] It is true, as was pointed out in the Minority Report, that this rule was an advance on the current practice of local authorities.

and that a maximum capital sum might be fixed above which benefit would not be payable.[1] The Minority justified the neglect of sums below a certain amount by the fact that this obviated "the necessity for investigation into small incomings", and because under the non-contributory pensions scheme an annual income equivalent to 50*s*. a week (of which not more than £1 a week should be earnings) is ignored. It was stated that an even higher limit might be appropriate for the unemployed "as the payment to them would as a rule be temporary only and they would contribute again to the Fund in due course".

We suggest that in the assessment of needs: (i) the interest, if any, derived from capital assets of all kinds should be completely ignored up to a certain limit of capital value, which limit should be considerably higher than the present one; and (ii) that above this limit of capital value the interest should be taken into account, on the basis of an assumed interest rate which progressively increased until it resulted in a certain amount of liquidation.

We make the first proposal because (*a*) it is extremely undesirable to penalise the small-

[1] p. 439.

scale personal thrift of the U.A.B.'s applicants; (*b*) we wish to simplify the operation of the means test, particularly as such a large proportion of the U.A.B.'s applicants are relatively short-period unemployed; (*c*) the actual income derived from capital assets is, as we have shown, a very small proportion of the income derived from all resources; (*d*) we do not believe that the unemployed would feel that this operated unfairly as between those of them who had, and those of them who had not, got capital resources.

We make the second proposal not because there are at present more than a negligible number of unemployed on the U.A.B. who possess capital resources of any kind,[1] but because it is desirable that the scope of the U.A.B. should be widened in two ways and should thus possibly include a certain number of individuals who are in possession of considerable assets. We are suggesting that non-manual workers whose rates of remuneration exceed £250 should be included in unemployment insurance (and consequently come under

[1] It is estimated by the Board that in December 1937 there were about 12,500 applicants (or their wives or husbands) who possessed capital resources other than that represented by the house which the applicant owned and occupied, and that the value of this capital was about £1,250,000.

Part II of the Act),[1] and that the remainder of the able-bodied unemployed should be transferred from public assistance to the U.A.B.[2] The latter will include a certain proportion of persons who had previously been working on their own account, for whom an upper limit is absolutely essential if there are not to be continual allegations by all concerned of abuse of State funds.

It is not possible to calculate with any accuracy the annual cost of abolition of the *household* means test. The Board estimated that in 1937 about £5 million out of the total of the resources possessed by applicants and the members of their households [3] was regarded as available to meet the needs of the household. The following table shows that even if the total value of the income derived from all the resources possessed by the applicant and his wife were taken into account under our proposed personal means test the figure corresponding to £5 million would, at that date, have been £3,662,000,[4] plus the

[1] See Chap. 5. [2] See Chap. 6.

[3] Only a small proportion of this total consists of resources owned by wives. See P. Ford, *Incomes, Means Tests and Personal Responsibility*, p. 47.

[4] This neglects the resources possessed by the applicant's dependants, other than his wife, although they would come under the personal means test. But the value of their resources would be very small.

value of the resources possessed by the new applicants who had previously been unemployed but not in receipt of an allowance. In practice, of course, the sum would be far less than this, and if we were reckoning the saving to the Exchequer there would have to be deducted from it the saving in administrative costs that would be involved, though there would, of course, also be some extra administrative costs due to the new applicants.

TABLE 14

ESTIMATED ANNUAL VALUE OF RESOURCES POSSESSED BY U.A.B. APPLICANTS [1] AND MEMBERS OF THEIR HOUSEHOLDS IN DECEMBER 1937

	Applicants	*Husbands (or wives)*	*Applicants plus husbands (or wives)*	*Total household resources*
Not earnings .	£1,482,000	£369,000	£1,851,000	£5,239,000
Earnings . .	£1,171,000	£640,000	£1,811,000	£13,675,000
Total	£2,653,000	£1,009,000	£3,662,000	£18,914,000

[1] Derived from Report of U.A.B. for 1937, p. 190. The unemployment insurance benefit that is being paid to those receiving supplementation allowances from the Board has been omitted from the table, since it makes up a large proportion of the total resources of applicants, and its inclusion gives a false impression of the resources possessed by applicants who are wholly supported by the Board.

CHAPTER 14

SUPPLEMENTATION OF UNEMPLOYMENT INSURANCE BENEFIT

THE Unemployment Assistance Board, like public assistance, is a service that supplements other forms of social service income. But while such supplementation is a very important function of the P.A.C., it is an unimportant function of the U.A.B., merely taking the form of the payment of supplementary allowances to certain of those in receipt of unemployment insurance benefit when assistance would, if it were payable, exceed benefit in amount. Nevertheless the existence of supplementation emphasises the difficulties connected with our system of social services; and in this particular case it provides the only direct and formal link (apart from the administrative one) between insurance and the assistance services. The longer our social services persist in their present form the more important supplementation will become. But this is not at all a satisfactory position, because the administrative expenses involved in making two separate cash payments to the same individual are naturally very high; it is most inconvenient for the applicant to make two separate applications; and it involves the insured person in the humiliation of having to submit to a means test.[1]

Supplementation of unemployment insurance benefit only became payable on the second appointed day, 1 April 1937. Eligible for it are those who, in the words of the Board's Report, "find that the amount of benefit is insufficient to meet their needs".[2] This means that (the Board assuming, of course, that its allowances are an accurate measure of an applicant's needs) supplementation may be payable if the allowance that the applicant would get were he on the U.A.B. exceeds what he does get in the form of benefit. This hypothetical allowance, like all allowances, depends upon the applicant's resources. But this is not to say that the granting of a supplementary allowance follows auto-

[1] In discussing the appropriate benefit rates for agricultural workers the Statutory Committee referred to the undesirability of widespread supplementation. *Report of U.I.S.C. on the question of the Insurance against Unemployment of Persons engaged in Employment in Agriculture, 1935.*

[2] Report of U.A.B. for 1937, p. 30.

matically upon the proof of need. It is, in fact, normally only given after four weeks of unemployment have elapsed, on the assumption that the applicant ought to have been able to save up sufficient to see him through such a short period.[1] It is extremely doubtful whether such a practice is consistent with the Board's obligation to relieve need. Nor would the allowance be given if it would only amount to 2*s*. or less—though the same is true in this case of the granting of ordinary allowances. Hardly any single men are in receipt of supplementation.

A very large proportion of supplementation cases arise because of high rent; some cases arise from the existence of more than one adult dependant in the household; and some from the existence of large families of children, and from special needs associated with sickness. But this, as will be seen, does not mean that supplementation is actually received in all those cases where one of these types of need exists; nor does it mean that more than a very small proportion of the unemployed with high rents get their rights.

[1] In deciding whether to grant supplementation within this period the rate of wages and the length of the previous spell of unemployment may be taken into account, or even the employment record over the whole of the last year.

The table[1] on page 171 shows what a great difference there is between the high rent area of London and the rest of the country in the amount of supplementation granted relatively to the unemployed population.[2] It also brings out the relatively high number of supplementations in South Wales,[3] and the extremely low number in Scotland—a total of 266 cases in the five administrative areas. In fact, outside London the power to grant supplementation has remained almost unused; and the cases in which it is granted will be regarded both by the Board, and by the insured population (in so far as it is conscious at all of their existence), as nothing but freaks.

But though high rents are the important factor, the number of supplementations increases considerably during the months in which winter allowances are paid, many of the supplementations being equivalent to winter allowances. The table on page 172 shows how the number of supplementations increases between

[1] Supplied by the Minister of Labour subsequently to a question asked in the House on 18 May 1939.

[2] The variation in proportion will in part be due to variations in the proportions of the Live Register on unemployment insurance.

[3] Probably due to political activity or awareness.

TABLE 15

District		*Numbers of unemployed persons on the registers of employment exchanges*	*Numbers of persons on the register with applications authorised for allowances in supplementation of Insurance benefit, 12 June 1939*	*Number of supplementations per 1000 unemployed persons*
London I	.	82,830	2,076	25·1
London II	.	86,944	2,448	28·2
London III	.	72,617	1,026	14·1
Norwich .	.	22,312	73	3·3
Bristol .	.	45,301	89	2·0
Birmingham	.	55,781	117	2·1
Hanley .	.	40,601	55	1·3
Nottingham	.	47,688	107	2·2
Leeds .	.	87,001	105	1·2
Sheffield .	.	63,563	138	2·2
Liverpool	.	84,531	199	2·3
Preston .	.	58,620	154	2·6
Manchester I	.	70,274	221	3·2
Manchester II	.	78,190	184	2·4
Carlisle .	.	15,537	59	3·8
Durham .	.	40,808	169	4·1
Middlesbrough	.	29,387	86	2·9
Newcastle-on-Tyne .	.	54,324	110	2·0
Dundee .	.	33,652	21	0·6
Edinburgh	.	33,444	47	1·4
Glasgow I	.	76,270	138	1·8
Glasgow II	.	47,972	58	1·2
Inverness	.	7,429	2	0·3
Cardiff .	.	40,290	282	7·0
Newport	.	23,236	165	7·1
Wrexham	.	18,828	48	2·5
Swansea .	.	32,149	142	4·4
Great Britain	.	1,349,579	8,319	6·2
Great Britain excluding London	.	1,107,188	2,769	2·5

November and April, and indicates also the general tendency to increase, despite the fall that has occurred in the number of unemployed.

TABLE 16

NUMBER OF CASES OF SUPPLEMENTATION OF UNEMPLOYMENT INSURANCE BENEFIT

Month	*1937* *	*1938* †	*1939* ‡
January		8,202	14,919
February		9,230	15,843
March		9,084	14,343
April	2,204	8,376	12,034
May	2,069	7,950	9,808
June	1,999	6,990	8,319
July	2,015	6,781	6,876
August	2,171	6,427	6,063
September	2,332	6,861	— §
October	3,095	7,673	
November	4,531	10,617	
December	6,525	13,763	

* Figures from Report of U.A.B. for 1937. Averages for one week.

† Ditto, 1938.

‡ From Ministry of Labour Gazette, relating to a particular day in each month.

§ Figures no longer published owing to the war.

The average size of supplementation varies slightly from month to month, being highest during the months when winter allowances are being paid. In December 1938 the average allowance paid to men was 7*s.* 9·7*d.*; to women 6*s.* 5*d.* It can be said that if supplementary allowances are granted at all the amount paid is substantial.

Previously to the second appointed day supplementary out-relief was given by the P.A.C. to certain cases on insurance benefit. When the Board took over this function it was considered that as the number of such cases had been very small, the ordinary applicant *ought* to be able to manage on his benefit alone, and cases of supplementation would continue to be "exceptional". Though it cannot be said that the Board actively resisted supplementing benefit, it has done very little to encourage applicants, and the majority of insured persons are certainly still ignorant of their rights. For the smallness of the numbers, particularly outside London, is to a large extent the consequence of ignorance, and despite continual questions in the House, there is still no poster in employment exchanges putting the position in plain terms. It is well known that the number of supplementation cases is greatest where workers' organisations are strongest, and this is simply because applicants are more likely to be aware of their rights. Also the tendency to apply depends to some extent upon the previous practice of the local public assistance authority. An applicant who has once received supplementation will be conscious of his rights when he is again unemployed, and for this reason alone the number will increase as time goes by.

The difficulty is that the Ministry of Labour does not feel it its duty to inform the applicant of his supplementation rights, and the U.A.B. takes no active steps to do so. The U.A.B. is associated in applicants' minds with the exhaustion of benefit rights, and unlike the P.A.C. it is not generally known as a supplementation service. As the Board has been specifically given the task of relieving the needs of the unemployed (and the *insured* unemployed as well as those who have exhausted their insurance rights), it should regard it as its positive duty to give assistance to all those who are in need owing to unemployment. Perhaps it is true that no social service should be expected to have the machinery for seeking out the individuals who are eligible for benefit or assistance but who do not in fact apply,[1] but owing to the close administrative co-operation between the Ministry of Labour and the Board,[2] it is not in this case a question of angling for applicants but merely of

[1] The question as to how far the State should compel the individual to make full use of the available social services might be important under socialism.

[2] U.A.B. allowances are of course paid through Ministry of Labour Employment Exchanges.

informing the unemployed as a matter of course that they may be in a position to receive additions to their benefit. The U.A.B. does not fulfil its obligations merely by granting supplementations to a few enlightened and persistent applicants.

CHAPTER 15

UNEMPLOYMENT ASSISTANCE BOARD WINTER ALLOWANCES

THE Unemployment Assistance Board began to give regular winter allowances in November 1937. The additions were given on account not only of increased need during winter but also of the rise in the prices of commodities, and they were regarded as discretionary increases to meet special circumstances. The officers of the Board were instructed to consider cases as they fell due for review, and to give special attention to "households where a substantial part, say not less than half, of the total household income is represented by the allowance from the Board". It was stated that, while all the circumstances of the case should be taken into account, "the Board expect that in many households an addition of two or three shillings would meet the requirements if the household is of normal size and composition". It was later added that persons living alone were in a position to receive allowances if they incurred direct expenditure upon fuel and light. At the end of the year approximately 263,000 unemployed, or 43% of the Board's applicants, were in receipt of winter allowances,[1] and the cost was £26,000 weekly,[2] or about 2*s.* per applicant.

In July 1938 new draft regulations were introduced to enable the Board to grant general additions to allowances in appropriate cases on account of winter conditions as such. The Board had apparently become rather doubtful as to the legality of granting additions on such a widespread scale under their general discretionary powers; and, it may be added, the Treasury rather anxious about their loss of control. But it is an odd regulation, part discretionary part not, since nothing is laid down about who is and who is not eligible to receive allowances. And, as Mr. Macmillan put it in the course of the debate in the House, it is difficult to see why such a regulation was necessary.[3]

[1] Report of U.A.B. for 1937, p. 23.
[2] Stated in the House of Commons, 18 July 1938.
[3] "If the Regulation has any legal meaning, which I very much doubt, let the House pass it, but it is the duty of the Board, whether the Regulation is passed or not, to meet the needs for assistance of the applicants who come before it."

Although there was no fixed scale of winter allowances, the following suggestions were made by the Board for the guidance of officers:

	Weekly addition *s.*	*d.*
Single person	1	0
Man and wife	2	0
Man and wife and one child	2	0
Up to three children	2	6
More than three children	3	0

In certain exceptional cases larger sums were granted, but it was only very rarely indeed that these exceeded 4*s*.

There can be no doubt as to the arbitrary application of the regulation. From information supplied on three occasions in December 1938 in answer to questions in the House, it is possible to calculate the proportion of current assessments which include an additional winter allowance for thirty-seven separate areas (including Great Britain as a whole). Just over one half of all the applicants in receipt of allowances in Great Britain were in receipt of winter allowances (51%). But this percentage varied from 39% (Newton) to 70% (Swansea II), and the other areas were distributed much more evenly than might be expected between these two extremes. The Minister of Labour has explained[1] that this variation in proportion is "principally due to differences in local conditions"—i.e. presumably to differences in types of applicants. But this explanation would hardly seem to be consistent with the fact that the average weekly value of the additions in the thirty-seven areas for which we have information only fell to 2*s.* in a single instance and never rose above 2*s.* 3*d.* Is this sufficiently explained by households of five invariably being in a small minority?

It had been hoped by some that the regulation would have the effect of "undoing the evils of the wage stop during winter".[2] But that this was a false hope is shown from the following quotation which occurred in a letter from the Minister of Labour to Mr. Whiteley at the end of 1938: "The Board do not feel that the winter allowances regulation should be so applied as to defeat the obvious purpose of this (the wages stop) provision." Most of those coming under the wages stop provision will be applicants with high rents and young families, so that they should be eligible for winter allowances; as it is,

[1] 22 December 1938.

[2] Mr. Lawson, in the course of the debate on the new Regulation.

they receive the same allowance in winter as in summer.

The National Unemployed Workers' Movement are very critical of the operation of the winter allowances regulation, and particularly of the failure of the Board to make the unemployed familiar with their rights. Although the Board stated that individual application for winter allowances would be unnecessary, as the merits of each case would be considered in the automatic reviews at the beginning of the winter, the N.U.W.M. state that thousands of special applications have had to be made, and that when they have taken up cases they have often been successful in getting allowances granted. The Board prides itself that only 647 appeals were made against refusals to grant winter allowances. But the N.U.W.M. state that the Board did not issue new determinations when cases were reviewed at the beginning of the winter, and that unless a new determination is issued, or an applicant himself makes a fresh application, he cannot appeal. This is true, although all determinations are reviewed over the month previous to the date on which allowances are first paid (so that the whole operates on a certain date), and although there are special facilities for appeal. But as the applicant is not informed of the decision not to grant him an allowance, he is often ignorant of what has been denied him. This is particularly important when new circumstances arise.

But the most serious feature of all is the shortness of the winter period, which began on 14 November 1938 and ended on 15 April 1939.[1] Does the Board seriously consider that no fires are necessary outside this period, and is Lord Rushcliffe's home unheated in the middle of October? Payments ought certainly to be made from the middle of October to the end of April. And anyway, as the N.U.W.M. ask, was the Board entitled from the purely legal angle to define the dates of the beginning and end of winter?

[1] On 5 October 1939 the Minister of Labour stated in the House that winter allowances would be payable as from 30 October 1939.

CHAPTER 16

UNEMPLOYMENT EXPENDITURE AND THE TRADE CYCLE

THE detailed discussion of the two unemployment services having been completed, we will now turn to the very important general question of co-ordination of unemployment policy and financial policy. This book is concerned with the relief and not the cure of unemployment, so there is no discussion of the possibilities of increasing employment through forms of public investment, other than rearmament. Even so it should be emphasised as strongly as possible, first, that a Labour Government would endeavour to keep unemployment within manageable limits through a policy of public loan expenditure (and rearmament would not be the only possible form of peace-time public loan expenditure as under the National Government), and second, that unemployment expenditure has in itself an effect on the degree of unemployment.[1]

Although the Statutory Committee is pledged to preserve the solvency of the Fund, and to pay off the whole of the existent debt by 1971, nevertheless, as explained in its Report for 1938,[2] it has certain borrowing powers. Section 60 of the 1935 Unemployment Act provides for short borrowing, and there are strict provisions for repayment. Under the 1938 Act there is provision for long borrowing, any sums advanced having to be repaid by terminable annuities ending in March 1971.[3] The amount that can be borrowed under this latter provision is limited to the differences between the actual amount of the debt at any moment and the amount which it would have been if payments towards its reduction had not been made under the 1938 Act.[4] As the debt was reduced by £20 million under this Act in 1938, the long-term

[1] By "unemployment expenditure" is meant expenditure on insurance benefit plus expenditure on unemployment allowances. The effect will be greater the lower the proportion of the unemployment expenditure that goes in administration.

[2] p. 14.

[3] The same date by which the whole debt has to be paid off.

[4] See p. 96.

borrowing powers of the Fund are already considerable, although the extent to which they would be used is doubtful, particularly as it might be necessary to pay more than the rate of interest which applies to the existing debt—viz. $3\frac{1}{8}\%$. The Statutory Committee holds the view that balances should be used to reduce debt "only to the extent that we may reasonably hope not to be forced later to borrow again, except for the short periods contemplated by the Act of 1938".[1]

It has already been shown that the Statutory Committee has been peculiarly bad at forecasting the future course of unemployment. For this reason it will have to adopt a new method of determining the Fund's disposable surplus. So far actual experience from year to year has been, without exception, more favourable than the expectation, and the Committee has been faced, on every occasion except in 1939, with the problem of disposing of unexpected surpluses. But if the Committee continues in its present methods it is just as likely to fall into the opposite error in future and to find itself faced with a deficit. It will certainly be made to appreciate the unreliability of future estimates

[1] Report of U.I.S.C. for 1937, p. 14.

of unemployment[1] when it is faced, in the middle of a depression, with only a small surplus in the Fund and the uncertainty (say) of whether recovery will begin in the next year or in the one after.[2]

What would the Statutory Committee do in these circumstances? Would it propose the cutting of benefit rates? It has already been pointed out that the Committee feels that any *increase* in benefit rates should only occur "as an act of deliberate social policy".[3] The Committee has not yet found it necessary to discuss the *reduction* of benefit rates, so it is not known whether it would find itself so helpless in the face of such a possibility. It is to be strongly suspected that in order to fulfil what it regards as its primary function of preserving the solvency of the Fund it would be willing to bear the responsibility of a reduction, despite the poverty that would result, and that in certain circumstances it would

[1] The Committee has already confessed that "we only prophesy because we must".

[2] Had the Statutory Committee existed at the beginning of 1932 it would have found it extremely difficult to decide at what date recovery should reasonably be expected to begin. In fact there was very little improvement in 1932 and expenditure on insurance benefit amounted to £57 million. When recovery did come in 1933, annual expenditure fell by about £14 million to £43 million.

[3] See p. 104.

be more likely to make such a proposal than to propose the raising of contributions. For employers' contributions are, and are even better known to be, a "tax on enterprise", and the employers' view weighs very heavily when employment is bad. The extent to which the Committee might be willing to borrow cannot even be surmised; we are very much hampered by the shortness of the period 1934 to 1939, from which we are compelled to take our evidence, and by its relative stability. The question of what the Statutory Committee *should* propose in times of trade depression will be considered later.

Next, to consider the Unemployment Assistance Board. It has two methods of varying its standard of assistance: through amending its regulations, or through a change in the exercise of its discretion. The 1934 Act does not prescribe the standard of assistance; but the Board is required to draw up its own regulations for the payment of allowances to applicants. These regulations do not have effect until they are first confirmed by the Minister and then approved by Parliament.[1] In Section 52 of the 1934 Act it

[1] Technically it is not necessary for Parliament to approve the rules. But either House can, within twenty-eight days after the rules have been confirmed by the Minister, resolve that they shall be annulled, thus rendering them void.

was laid down that the Board should submit its first regulations to the Minister within four months of the passing of the Act, and that the same should be done thereafter "from time to time as occasion may require". If the Minister refuses the Board's draft regulations and draws up his own instead, he has to "inform the Board of the variations and amendments which he intends to make and the Board shall report to him thereon and he shall consider the report". In such a case the Minister must also lay before Parliament a statement of his variations and amendments and the Board's report thereon, and the regulations must be approved by each House.

But although the regulations when drawn up take a very definite and elaborate form, they do not in themselves completely prescribe the standard of assistance. The average level of assistance can and does change without a change in the actual regulations, through a change in the exercise of discretion. The most important discretionary powers of the Board are the granting of additional or reduced allowances on account of what are called special circumstances or exceptional needs. "Special circumstances" are of a sufficiently permanent nature to take the form of an adjustment of the assessment for the scale allowance; "exceptional needs" refer to circumstances of a non-continuous character and generally involve a lump sum or non-recurrent grant.

Very little information relating to the treatment of special circumstances is available in the Reports of the Board. No statement has ever been made as to the average amount by which allowances are increased owing to the existence of special circumstances, or of the number of reductions.[1] At the end of 1936 there were about 115,000 discretionary increases in respect of special circumstances—that is, increases were granted to about 20% of the total number of applicants. No figures are given for 1937 or 1938—whether because they are unknown, or considered to be insufficiently interesting or important, or whether there is something to hide, can only be surmised.[2] The fact is (and this is most unsatisfactory) we know very little of the Board's long-period discretionary policy. We do

[1] The number of reductions on account of special circumstances have been "comparatively few in number". (1936 Report of the Board, p. 27.) Many of these would have been benefit suspended cases. See Appendix 3.

[2] Nor do any of the Regional Officers discuss such discretionary allowances in their separate reports.

know, though, that there is plenty of room for variation if need be.

During the year 1938 there were 20,141 grants made in respect of exceptional needs, as compared with 23,229 grants in 1937. Exceptional needs grants are sometimes made on loan, and such cases are presumably included in these figures, thus making them somewhat misleading. As it is estimated that 1¼ million different individuals applied to the Board in 1938,[1] only about 2% of them received grants in respect of exceptional needs.[2] In 1937 more than half the grants were of amounts under £1.

As has already been shown,[3] the U.A.B. also exerts its discretionary powers through the use of the wages stop regulation. The number of wages stop reductions is small, but the Board might very well choose to make it considerably larger.

In 1938 new draft regulations were introduced to enable the Board to grant additional allowances on account of winter conditions, and winter allowances ceased to be the discretionary increases they had been previously. Neverthe-

[1] Report of U.A.B. for 1938, p. 60.

[2] This makes no allowance for the same individual receiving more than one grant.

[3] See p. 44.

less, as is shown,[1] there remains a large element of what can only be called discretion in the administration of the regulation, and it is still reasonable to include the granting of winter allowances with the Board's other discretionary powers. Both the number and the size of winter additions can be varied at the will of the Board. The mere proof of actual additional winter needs is insufficient to bring about an increase in the allowance.

What will the Board do when faced with a severe depression? It is quite unrealistic to suppose that because it is an autonomous body,[2] independent of the Minister of Labour, or of anyone else, and charged with the function of relieving need arising from unemployment, therefore its standard of allowances will not change unless there is also a change in the standard of needs of the unemployed. Even if the Board itself could achieve the degree of detachment necessary for concentration on the

[1] See Chap. 15.

[2] The U.A.B. consists of a chairman, a deputy chairman, and not less than one nor more than four other members. At least one member of the Board must be a woman. At the present time Lord Rushcliffe is chairman, Miss Violet Markham deputy chairman, and there are three other members. The chairman is paid £5,000 per year, the deputy chairman £3,000, and the other members £750 each.

relief of the particular needs of the individual unemployed person, that would be insufficient. For the 1934 Act was not successful—perhaps fortunately—in removing the unemployed from politics. Experience at the beginning of 1935 merely mocked this suggestion. The original set of regulations were so rigid and so harsh in individual cases that in order to compel their reconsideration the machinery of democracy really came into play and unemployment went as deep into politics as ever before. It is true that less Parliamentary time is now spent than formerly in discussing unemployment problems;[1] but this is because the 1934 Act was the first piece of legislation to make absolutely permanent provision for the unemployed outside the insurance scheme, and not because of the autonomous position of the U.A.B. The Minister of Labour is as willing to answer U.A.B. as unemployment insurance questions in the House, merely prefacing his answers with such phrases as "I am informed that . . ."

It is certain that the Board would be a highly political topic in a time of trade depression; and

[1] Between 1920 and the passing of the 1934 Act there were thirty-five Acts of Parliament dealing with unemployment insurance.

partly because of this it is certain, too, that under a Government of the Right there would be at such a time a reduction in allowances. This would probably begin insidiously, working through the Board's discretionary powers. There would be an increase in the number of reductions in respect of special circumstances and a decrease in the number and amount of the increases. There would be more wages stop cases. There might even be a tightening up of the rent rules.[1] Only later would the drafting of a revised set of regulations be involved.[2]

And, in addition, the Board might reduce its expenditure by declaring some of those for whom it is already responsible to be outside scope as not being capable of, or available for, work. It is common knowledge that a consider-

[1] Rent rules were not discussed under the Board's discretionary powers above, owing to the importance of the advice given by the Advisory Committees in the original formulation of these rules, though these rules are not rigidly followed. See p. 31.

[2] The drafting of new regulations can only be initiated by the Board itself. But faced with any reluctance on the part of the Board it is difficult to believe that the present Government would not provoke it to action if (say) the rate of unemployment increased so that the Board's annual expenditure rose from £40 million to £80 million. A body spending Treasury money at the rate at which it is spent by the Board cannot be independent of the Government in any really important sense.

able number of the Board's applicants are not, in any reasonable sense, capable of work. If they were new applicants, applying for allowances for the first time, they would be declared to be outside scope, for the Board is much stricter in its attitude to the "capability" and "availability" of new applicants than in its attitude to those for whom it has already accepted responsibility [1]—indeed it very seldom declares an applicant to be outside scope once he has been accepted. This is reasonable in so far as continuous living at the Board's low standard of living tends in itself to reduce "capability".

It appears, therefore, that in times of trade depression there is a very high risk that allowances would be reduced, although, as will be argued, it is particularly urgent at such times that more and not less money per head should be spent on the unemployed. In fixing the revised scale of allowances, it is doubtful whether the Board or the Government would take the level of unemployment insurance benefit into account. If they would, then, owing to the lesser flexibility of insurance benefits, the risks are not so great, though the Board would still be able to tighten up its discretionary policy. No

[1] See p. 76.

legislative provision, other than the fixing of a minimum scale of allowances, would remove this danger. It is only under a Labour Government that the risk of heavy cuts in allowances would cease to exist.

There is next the very important question of how the Statutory Committee and the Unemployment Assistance Board *ought* to behave in time of trade depression. We have seen that there is a chance that benefit rates and scale rates would be reduced, but it is certain that such reductions should only be made in the very last resort. There are two reasons for this, the most obvious one being the increased poverty that would result. A cut in rates might appear to be justified by a fall in the cost of living. But it would not be in fact, because unless there were a very large fall in the cost of living, benefits would still in many cases be insufficient to cover minimum needs. In addition, despite the rise in real (as distinct from money) benefits, the overlap question would be no more acute, since real wages and real benefits would rise together. Also there would be no guarantee at all that benefits would be restored to their old level when the cost of living rose again.

But reduction of benefits is also objectionable

because it is in itself bad for employment.[1] Even if the reduction were immediately reflected in decreased taxation this would be the case; and if it were reflected not in a reduction of taxation, but in a reduction of borrowing by the Unemployment Fund, the effect would be even worse. In either case the spending power of the lowest income group in the community would have been reduced relatively to the spending power of the rest of the community, and the distribution of the national income would have been made more uneven. The more uneven the distribution of income, the greater, in general, the amount of unemployment that is associated with any level of national income. A reduction of borrowing would be even worse for employment than a reduction in taxation because money that is borrowed would have been much less likely to have been spent and not saved than money that is removed by taxation. It is because the "rich" spend, on the average, a smaller proportion of their income than the "poor" that any

[1] It is unfortunately quite impossible adequately to justify this statement here, so that the unintelligibility of this paragraph to the majority of readers is unavoidable. See J. M. Keynes, *The General Theory of Employment, Interest and Money*, or Joan Robinson, *Introduction to the Theory of Employment*.

influence that tends to make the distribution of income more uneven tends also to increase unemployment. This all means that a cut in benefit rates increases the number as well as the poverty of the unemployed, and consequently produces less saving in unemployment expenditure than would appear at first sight.

An alternative to the reduction of benefit would be a reduction of the period for which benefit could be drawn. It has already been noticed that the Statutory Committee regards the question, in so far as large changes are involved, as a "broad issue of national policy",[1] and is therefore not very likely [2] to propose such changes. In considering the position no assumption will be made about the relative attractiveness to the unemployed person of being on the insurance scheme or the U.A.B.; the question will be considered simply from its financial aspect. Suppose that the Statutory Committee decided to propose the cutting down of the minimum period for which the insured person is entitled to benefit from six months to four months. Then the proportion of unemployment expenditure which was borne by the State would be increased, for the Board is financed

[1] See p. 107. [2] But see p. 108, footnote 2.

entirely by the Exchequer, and the insurance scheme by the three contributing parties. Whether the wage-earning class would benefit from this change would depend on what action would have been taken had the benefit period not been reduced. If contributions would otherwise have been increased, wage earners would benefit through being made responsible for a smaller proportion of total unemployment expenditure. But if, on the other hand, the Statutory Committee would have had to resort to borrowing, then, for reasons that have already been indicated, the shortening of the period of benefit would in itself be bad for employment. This is a dilemma that might have to be faced if a depression were really severe. On the one hand, it is desirable that the State should be responsible for as much as possible of the additional unemployment expenditure incurred during a depression; on the other hand, the loan method of finance has the most favourable effect on the volume of unemployment. There is a further consideration. Offsetting this advantage of loan expenditure is the disadvantage that a debt would be incurred that would have to be paid off in the future by insured persons. This consideration is probably not serious enough to outweigh the general case for borrowing as against taxation.

A further alternative is an increase in the rate of contribution. It is to be noticed that contribution income decreases with an increase in unemployment. The Statutory Committee cannot propose an increase in the State contribution without a corresponding increase in the contributions from the other two parties. Were such an increase to occur, therefore, it would have to be directly on the initiative of the Government, provoked or unprovoked by the Statutory Committee; and the National Government would, of course, be extremely unlikely to take such initiative.

There remains the possibility of raising employers' or employees' contributions. The contribution method of raising revenue has already been discussed.[1] Here it will only be added that the objections to taxing the worker in this way increase with the degree of unemployment. This is the case because: (1) The employed person (who pays contributions) is less well off owing (*a*) to the increased assistance he has to give, reluctantly or willingly, to his unemployed friends and relations; (*b*) to the increased chance

[1] See p. 19.

that previous or future unemployment will reduce his own resources; (2) employers' contributions have a more depressing effect on enterprise when unemployment is high. Offsetting these considerations is the fact of the rise in purchasing power consequent on the fall in food prices that usually occurs when there is increased unemployment.

The conclusion must be that the Statutory Committee should be prepared to use its borrowing powers, and to use them before it has exhausted all other possible methods of making the Fund solvent. The Committee must not regard itself as failing in the impossible duty of forecasting future unemployment if borrowing is occasionally found to be necessary—even if this is long- and not short-term borrowing. As a Labour Government would resist any proposed cuts in benefit the Statutory Committee might then, at times, be compelled to resort to borrowing.

But when the Statutory Committee comes to make its next Report it is likely to be faced with very different problems from those we have just been considering. For the Unemployment Fund is now running up a surplus at such a great rate that the Committee may even find it difficult to know how to dispose of it. For the twenty-six weeks between 1 April and 30 September 1939 the income of the Unemployment Fund exceeded its expenditure by £12 million, and as the war is likely to have a favourable effect on unemployment the surplus for the present financial year may well exceed £20 million. In discussing what the Committee ought to do with a sum of this magnitude we are concerning ourselves with absolutely immediate problems and not, as elsewhere, with Labour Party policy.

It has been seen that the present Statutory Committee, under the present Government, is, other things equal, unlikely to propose benefit rate increases, although, despite the low level of wages, there is still room for such increases.[1] It will probably, therefore, repeat its recent policy of debt repayment; [2] and faced, in addition, with the prospect of a similar surplus in the following year, it would be likely to reduce contribution rates, particularly as the repayment of debt would in itself result in an additional disposable surplus. It would not be in a position to increase the number of additional days of

[1] But see p. 108, footnote 2.

[2] Unless by any chance it adopts the proposal for a third-child family allowance scheme to be financed out of the unemployment fund. See p. 115.

benefit for contributors with good employment records, as under the Unemployment (Emergency Powers) Act no such additional days are allowed. It is therefore perhaps fortunate for the Statutory Committee in its present position that the Unemployment Fund was made responsible for paying off a debt of £106 million. Were debt repayment not a possibility, the Statutory Committee would be more likely to devise methods of spending its money.

BRIEF SUMMARY OF THE MORE IMPORTANT PROPOSALS AND CONCLUSIONS[1]

I. The dual system of unemployment insurance and unemployment assistance should be maintained (pp. 10–26).

II. *Unemployment Insurance.*

(1) The possibility of varying the worker's contribution (but not benefit) with the wage rate should be examined (pp. 22–25). The contribution method of raising revenue is most unsatisfactory both because the employer's contribution is liable to be passed on to the worker and because it involves a regressive form of taxation on the worker. In the long run the method of financing the social insurances requires reconsideration (p. 26).

(2) The general level of benefit rates urgently requires increasing, as many unemployed are at present compelled to live below the subsistence

[1] This summary makes no attempt at completeness.

level. As the largest families are relatively much the poorest, the first instalment of this increase should come through raising the child dependants' rate (p. 30).

(3) The overlap of benefit on wages is not yet so serious as to provide grounds for opposing any further increase in benefit rates, but a point will soon be reached where benefit increases will have to wait on the raising of the wage level, through, in particular, the introduction of family allowances (pp. 40–44).

(4) Non-manual workers, working under a contract of employment, whose rates of remuneration exceed £250 per year, should be included within the scope of the scheme (pp. 55–60).

(5) The Unemployment Insurance Statutory Committee is in fact reaching the limit of the proposals that it is prepared to make on its own responsibility to improve the insurance scheme, so that even if there were a large surplus in the Fund, then, if there were not changes elsewhere, it is doubtful whether benefit rates would be increased. The Committee should concentrate on the state of the Fund and the most urgent needs of the unemployed and should ignore, as far as possible, the indirect conse-

quences of its proposals. Parliament should accept its responsibility as the only body at present capable of co-ordinating the social services (p. 111). The Statutory Committee has not proved at all successful in forecasting future unemployment (pp. 92–98). The Unemployment Fund Debt should be transferred from the Unemployment Fund to the Exchequer (pp. 98–103).

(6) The child dependants' rate should be increased from 3*s*. to 5*s*. (pp. 112–117). The possibility of financing out of the Unemployment Fund a third child family allowance scheme for all insured workers should be considered (pp. 115–117).

(7) The position of women relative to men should be improved either by reducing their contribution rate or by increasing their benefit rate (pp. 118–125).

(8) The Anomalies (Married Women) Order should be repealed (pp. 126–137).

(9) The waiting period should be abolished for all those who are unemployed for three days or longer (pp. 138–144).

III. *Unemployment Assistance.*

(10) Scale rates require increasing, for in a large proportion of cases allowances are in-

sufficient to cover absolute minimum needs. Ultimately such increases must wait on rises in the wage level. (See (2) and (3) above. Pp. 31–33.)

(11) The wages stop regulation should be abolished (pp. 44–48).

(12) All the able-bodied unemployed still remaining on public assistance should be transferred to the Board (pp. 61–77).

(13) In drawing up the scale rates there is evidence that a minimum standard of assistance from other social services was assumed, and the absence of this should be regarded as evidence of the existence of special circumstances (p. 87).

(14) The household means test should be abolished and a personal means test, applying to the applicant and his dependants (in respect of whom an addition is made to the allowance), and normally not involving home investigation but a mere declaration of income, should be substituted for it. More favourable and more consistent treatment should be given to applicants' resources, particularly to capital assets (pp. 145–166).

(15) Increased publicity should be given to the power to grant supplementation of unemployment benefit (p. 173).

(16) The period during which winter allowances are paid should be extended (p. 181).

Unemployment expenditure has, in itself, an effect upon the level of unemployment, so that it is important that it should be related to trade-cycle policy. Benefits and allowances should on no account be reduced in times of trade depression, either directly, or, as in the case of the Board, through the tightening up of the discretionary policy. The Statutory Committee should not hesitate to go in for long-term borrowing if necessary (pp. 182–201).

APPENDIX I

A COMPARISON OF AVERAGE PAYMENTS OF INSURANCE BENEFIT WITH AVERAGE U.A.B. ALLOWANCES

THE Board's scale rates were fixed without any precise reference being made to the prevailing level of unemployment insurance benefit rates;[1] nor, since the Board is concerned to relieve need, should it have been deflected by such outside considerations. Nevertheless, it is certain that the general level of benefit was borne in mind, if only because the Board had a duty to supplement benefit where it was insufficient to cover needs.

But there are two provisions, not yet, at any rate, of great importance, which tend to make the actual payments equal in individual cases. These are supplementation of insurance benefit by the U.A.B.[2] and what is known as the "benefit rate fall back". The latter is a surprising provision which was introduced for the first time in the U.A.B.'s revised regulations. It lays down that a worker who is at the head of a household, and who has dependants and no available resources, shall receive not less than his appropriate benefit rate—industrial or agricultural. This appropriate benefit

[1] See p. 33 of the First Report of the U.A.B.

[2] See Chap. 14.

rate is, most oddly, not the current benefit rate but the benefit rate in 1936.[1] The provision applies whether or not the applicant has ever been eligible for insurance benefit. Despite a question to the Minister of Labour in the House, no indication has ever been given of the number of such cases, but it is supposedly very small.[2]

The following information relating to average payments of unemployment benefit has been supplied by the Ministry of Labour:

	Males		*Females*	
	s.	*d.*	*s.*	*d.*
(1) 1937	19	4	11	9
(2) January–March 1938 . .	19	7	11	6
(3) April–December 1938. .	19	0	11	7

Before the corresponding figures for average allowances are given, mention will be made of the reasons for their lack of comparability with the average benefit figures.

(i) Both sets of figures represent not average amounts paid in respect of complete weeks of unemployment but average amounts *per payment*. The number of days in a week in respect of which a payment can be made varies from one to six. It is evident that changes in the number of days for which payments are made has an

[1] The National Unemployed Workers' Movement point out that there is no justification for this date in the Regulations, where reference is simply made to the "appropriate benefit rate". On the other hand the Board's Explanatory Memorandum on the Unemployment Assistance Draft Regulations makes reference to the benefit which the applicant would "under present law" receive.

[2] Under the Board's amended regulations (December 1939), the same increase will be made to the allowance as before, despite the rise in scale rates.

appreciable effect on the average benefit or allowance. For the average figure for males in row (3) above was less than the average figure in row (2), despite the fact that adult dependants' benefit was increased from 9*s.* to 10*s.* at the end of March 1938. This must have been due to an increase in the proportion of persons unemployed for very short periods. The benefit figures will be more depressed than the allowance figures by payments made in respect of incomplete weeks of unemployment, as the majority of intermittent workers retain their insurance rights.

(ii) Applicants for assistance, as compared with applicants for benefit, include a larger proportion of those over twenty-one; also there are general reasons for supposing that a higher proportion of the Board's adult men has dependants. The following figures (the only ones that seem to be available) do not prove this latter statement, but are given for what they are worth:

Class	*Number of men applicants*	*Number of dependent children*	*Number of dependent children per applicant*
Unemployment Insurance Benefit * 1931 . .	3,268	7,353	2·25
U.A.B. Allowances † 1937 .	245,540	578,530	2·35

* From the Ministry of Labour's Evidence to the Royal Commission on Unemployment Insurance.

† From Report of U.A.B. for 1937, p. 83.

The figures of average allowances are:

	Males		*Females*	
	s.	*d.*	*s.*	*d.*
1937	24	11	13	8
January–March 1938 . .	25	6	13	1
April–December 1938 . .	24	7	13	1

Despite considerations (i) and (ii) above, it appears justifiable to conclude that allowances would, on the average, exceed benefit, even if the populations of the two services were precisely similar, and that in any case a substantial proportion of applicants gain, or would gain, an advantage from the exhaustion of their insurance rights.[1] The amount by which average allowances exceed average benefit increases when winter allowances are being paid; and this is reflected in an increased number of supplementation cases.[2]

One of the results of the discrepancy between the two sets of rates is that unemployment allowances are sometimes reduced because of the existence of a person in receipt of benefit in the same household. A man in receipt of 27*s*. from the U.A.B. in respect of himself and his wife, might very well have his allowance reduced to 21*s*. because of an unemployed son in receipt of 17*s*. benefit coming into the same household.[3]

Even if a more conclusive comparison were possible it could not be said that an increase in U.A.B. scale rates is less urgently required than an increase in insurance benefit rates, for, as has already been pointed out, the needs of an unemployment person increase with the period of unemployment. It is certain that *both* benefit rates and scale rates require increasing.

[1] Now that scale rates have risen (December 1939), this is truer than previously. But the Statutory Committee is likely to propose the raising of benefit rates in its next report.

[2] See p. 171. [3] Hansard, 6 December 1938.

APPENDIX 2

SHORT-TIME WORKING AND THE CONTINUITY RULE

UNDER the continuity rule separate spells of unemployment may be linked together either backwards or forwards to form a continuous period of unemployment for the purpose of counting as waiting days or for the payment of benefit. Any three days of unemployment in six consecutive days, excluding Sundays, are regarded as continuous (the three-in-six rule); isolated days that do not form part of a continuous spell are not valid for waiting day purposes, and no benefit is payable in respect of them.

The three-in-six rule is in some ways most unsatisfactory. A man who is unemployed regularly on the same two days a week will never receive any benefit, for there will be no period of six consecutive days in which there are three days of unemployment. This means that a considerable amount of regular unemployment goes unpaid. Another man who is unemployed to the same extent, but whose days of unemployment are differently distributed, may receive benefit in respect of all his individual days of unemployment. The following diagrams illustrate first the case of a man who was unemployed on the average for two days per week, and who received benefit for each of these days, and second the case of a man who was unemployed every Wednesday and Thursday and received no benefit at all. The X's represent days of unemployment, the O's days of employment.

THE EXPERIENCE OF ONE APPLICANT OVER SIX WEEKS

Number of week	*Wednesday*	*Thursday*	*Friday*	*Saturday*	*Monday*	*Tuesday*	*Days*	
							Paid	*Signed*
1 .	O	O	O	X	X	O	—	2
2 .	O	O	X	X	O	O	4	2
3 .	O	X	O	X	O	O	1	2
4 .	O	X	X	O	O	O	3	2
5 .	O	O	O	O	X	X	—	2
6 .	X	X	O	O	O	O	4	2
						Total	12	12

THE EXPERIENCE OF ANOTHER APPLICANT

Number of week	*Wednesday*	*Thursday*	*Friday*	*Saturday*	*Monday*	*Tuesday*	*Days*	
							Paid	*Signed*
1 .	X	X	O	O	O	O	—	2
2 .	X	X	O	O	O	O	—	2
3 .	X	X	O	O	O	O	—	2

Explanation of the first diagram: In the first week no benefit is payable because the total number of days of unemployment is less than three. In the second week benefit is payable in respect of four days, since Saturday and Monday of week 1, together with Friday of week 2, make up a period of continuous unemployment, and Saturday of week 2 can be similarly connected with the previous Friday and Monday. In the third week benefit is payable in respect of the single day Thursday—which connects up with the previous Friday and Saturday, but no benefit is payable in respect of the Saturday. However, in the fourth week, the Thursday and Friday are days of unemployment, and these, together with this previous Saturday, form a further continuous period of three days.

It is usual in connection with the short-time question to discuss the extent to which the present continuity rule leads to so-called abuse of the Unemployment Fund—particularly in the dock industry [1]—and the general question of the use of the Unemployment Fund for the finance of short-period unemployment. There are three separate and relevant questions: (*a*) The degree to which employers take deliberate advantage of the continuity rule by putting workers on short time when they would hesitate to do so otherwise. (*b*) The degree to which (i) workers adjust the spells of their employment in accordance with the continuity rule; (ii) workers and employers co-operate so that the maximum may be drawn out of the Fund. (*c*) The social advantages and disadvantages of the spreading of unemployment through short-time working. Sufficient information does not exist to answer these questions completely. But it may be commented that (*a*) some prosperous employers, notably in the motor industry, are undoubtedly more irresponsible about providing their workers with full-time employment

[1] This is such a large subject that it cannot be discussed here.

than they would be were it not possible to claim benefit for the odd days. But the following table shows what a small proportion of total days of unemployment consist of short spells, and therefore that such employers are not seriously ''abusing' 'the Fund; though this is not to say that their workers are not suffering hardship through their inability to claim benefit.

MEN ON STANDARD BENEFIT—2 FEBRUARY 1931 [1]

Length of spell in days	*Percentage of total number of spells of unemployment*	*Percentage of aggregate days of unemployment in spells of various lengths*
1	26·4	1·7
2	12·6	1·6
3	13·4	2·6
4–6	15·2	4·8

And (*b*) instances are known in which the conditions of work are regulated to allow the workers to draw the maximum out of the Fund. This must not be thought of as benefiting employers only.

[1] See *Ministry of Labour Gazette*, August 1932. Unfortunately, information for a later date is not available.

APPENDIX 3

DISQUALIFICATIONS AND THE UNEMPLOYMENT ASSISTANCE BOARD

THOSE who are disqualified for short periods from receiving unemployment benefit are eligible to receive allowances from the Unemployment Assistance Board, unless their disqualification is the result of a trade dispute. The number of disqualified persons in receipt of assistance is quite substantial, fluctuates heavily from month to month, and is showing a definite tendency to increase. The following table illustrates this:

	Number in receipt of allowances who are disqualified for short periods from receiving benefit
June 1937	1,577
September 1937	1,705
December 1937	4,989
March 1938	5,599
June 1938	3,147
September 1938	2,957
December 1938	7,158
March 1939	7,529

From information supplied by the Board relating to the year 1938 it appears that 7·3% of the total number of new applicants to the Board had been suspended from unemployment benefit pending a decision from the Court of Referees, and a further 0·9% had been definitely disqualified from unemployment benefit.[1] Therefore, on the average, 8·2% of the total of new applicants to the Board at any one time were applying for assistance because they had been disqualified or suspended from benefit. This percentage can be compared with 32·9% who come on to the Board immediately on exhausting their unemployment benefit. A small proportion of those suspended from benefit would later have their rights restored as a result of the appeal, so that the actual number maintained by the Board would fall slightly below 8·2%. But it is clear that in numbers alone this is a very important class of applicant.

Applicants are disqualified for: (i) leaving employment voluntarily without just cause, (ii) failure or refusal to apply for, or accept, suitable employment, or failure to carry out written directions, (iii) unemployment that results from a stoppage due to a trade dispute, (iv) unemployment that is due to misconduct. In all these cases, except the third (disqualification due to a trade dispute), application may be made to the Board for the period of disqualification, which will be of any length up to six weeks. But many disqualified persons are unaware that they may claim allowances: and, again, it is no one's duty to inform them.

The following table shows that the increase in the number of U.A.B. applicants who have been disqualified from benefit cannot be entirely ascribed to an increase in the total number of disqualifications. The table is derived from information given monthly in the *Ministry of Labour Gazette*, and the resultant total

[1] The former percentage is much higher than the latter because the case has not usually been finally decided when application is first made to the Board.

number of disqualifications is only an estimate. The number of juveniles disallowed has been subtracted in order to obtain the figures in columns (1), (2) and (3), as juveniles aged fourteen to sixteen may not apply to the Board, and it is only rarely that those aged sixteen to eighteen will do so. Separate figures of juveniles and adults disqualified owing to trade disputes are not given. The final figures make no allowance for the very small number of decisions that are reversed on appeal to the Umpire.

NUMBER OF PERSONS DISQUALIFIED FROM RECEIVING INSURANCE BENEFIT

	Voluntary (1)	*Mis-conduct* (2)	*Refusal* (3)	*Trade Disputes* (4)	*Total*	*Total excluding* (4)
June 1937 .	10,985	4,196	3,236	4,714	24,131	19,417
September 1937	12,182	4,612	2,882	15,232	34,908	19,676
December 1937	8,692	4,020	2,909	4,817	20,438	15,621
March 1938 .	10,089	4,666	2,964	2,056	19,775	17,719
June 1938 .	9,032	3,749	2,652	6,037	21,470	15,433
September 1938	10,418	4,336	2,395	2,401	19,550	17,149
December 1938	8,156	3,655	2,759	1,441	16,011	14,570
March 1939 .	9,484	4,296	3,151	1,995	18,926	16,931

Reasons for disqualification:

(1) Employment left voluntarily.
(2) Employment lost owing to misconduct.
(3) Failure or refusal to apply for job, etc.
(4) Trade disputes.

In their Report for 1938 the Board makes reference to disqualification which has arisen from a man's own fault, and state that it "would obviously be against public policy to grant an allowance of such an amount or under such conditions as to make the suspension from benefit a matter of indifference to the applicant". Consequently recourse is made to the power to reduce allowances in cases of special circumstances. Surprisingly, no reference is made in the Report to the general increase in the number of disqualification cases. Perhaps the Board is uncertain of its attitude.

APPENDIX 4

A COMPARISON BETWEEN THE APPLICANTS FOR INSURANCE BENEFIT AND UNEMPLOYMENT ALLOWANCES

I. Periods of Unemployment.

LENGTH OF CURRENT SPELL OF UNEMPLOYMENT [1]

4 NOVEMBER 1939

	Less than 3 months	*3–6 months*	*6–12 months*	*More than 12 months*	*Total*
Percentage of U.A.B. applicants unemployed for various periods	28	10	16	45	100
Percentage of applicants for insurance benefit unemployed for various periods	82	10	6	3	100
Percentage of each group on U.A.B.	14	33	58	89	33

But this table is somewhat misleading, as an applicant who is unemployed for as short a time as four days will, however long his previous spell of unemployment, be moved down to the "less than three months" group. The following tables show the actual amount of em-

[1] A spell of unemployment is broken by employment lasting for more than three days.

ployment that U.A.B. applicants had in three years.[1] There is no corresponding information available for insurance applicants.

DURATION OF EMPLOYMENT OF U.A.B. APPLICANTS IN LAST THREE YEARS

	None	*Less than 6 months*	*6 months to 1 year*	*1–2 years*	*2 years or over*	*Total*
Males: Percentage in each group	34	37	14	11	3	100
Females: Percentage in each group	26	24	20	20	10	100

II. *Age of Applicants.*

PERCENTAGE OF UNEMPLOYED IN EACH AGE GROUP ON ALLOWANCES[2] (1 NOVEMBER 1937)

Age	*Men Percentage on allowances*	*Women Percentage on allowances*
18–20	23	15
21–24	36	11
25–34	43	12
35–44	52	20
45–54	55	31
55–59	59	40
60–64	66	52
Total	49	19

[1] From Report of U.A.B. for 1937, p. 65.
[2] Derived from *Ministry of Labour Gazette*, January 1938.

III. *Circumstances of Applicants immediately preceding their application to the Unemployment Assistance Board.*[1]

	Percentage of total number of applicants
Work *	35·0
Exhaustion of unemployment benefit	32·9
Sickness	4·9
Supplementation of unemployment benefit	6·2
Disqualified from unemployment benefit	0·9
Suspended from unemployment benefit	7·3
Other circumstances	12·8

* Including service in H.M. Forces.

IV. *Industry in which last employed.*

Figures of the proportion of the unemployed on benefit and assistance in each industry, in June 1936, are given in an article by Sir William Beveridge, "An Analysis of Unemployment".[2] The figures showed that a low rate of unemployment is not invariably associated with a high proportion of the unemployed on benefit and vice versa.

INDUSTRIES WITH LOW UNEMPLOYMENT AND HIGH PERCENTAGE OF TOTAL UNEMPLOYED ON ASSISTANCE

	Percentage of workers unemployed	*Percentage of unemployed on U.A.B.*
Average all industries	12·9	39·6
Gas, water and electricity supply	8·5	59·1
Railway service (non-permanent)	6·8	45·0
Chemicals	8·4	47·5
Railway carriages	4·6	47·8

[1] From information supplied by the Board, and based on examinations of 130,000 cases during 1938.

[2] *Economica*, November 1936.

Industries with High Unemployment and High Percentage of Total Unemployed on Benefit

	Percentage of workers unemployed	*Percentage of unemployed on benefit*
Average all industries	12·9	47·4
Tinplates	29·1	72·8
Fishing	18·2	61·5
Pottery, earthenware	19·5	71·2
Textile bleaching, etc.	18·1	75·7
Dock, harbour, river and land service	28·5	72·8

INDEX

n. refers to footnotes.